the yoga technique guide

principles of alignment and sequencing

By Bruce Bowditch
www.bruce–bowditch.com

Third Eye Press

ISBN: 978-0-9832367-2-6

Design by Melina Lew and illustration by Bruce Bowditch

This manual is intended for experienced yoga practitioners and teachers of yoga. It is offered as an aid in developing a home practice for students or as a sequencing guide for teachers of any style. It is not intended to teach the specifics of āsana technique; therefore the guidance of a qualified instructor is strongly encouraged. Before embarking on any āsana practice, consult with a qualified professional regarding any health issues, injuries or physical limitations.

Printed in China
By Prolong Press Ltd

www.bruce-bowditch.com

THIRD EYE PRESS

table of contents

alignment principles

table of contents
yoga sequencing

preface

I believe life can be better. I believe we can all live healthier, happier, more fulfilled lives. I believe we are never trapped in our past, or by our current circumstances, and that our future has no limits. We all have the possibility to heal, to grow, to achieve our dreams and realize our potential. If we allow our imagination to flourish, if we open ourselves to our deeper wisdom and allow our imaginings to blossom, anything is possible. We can transform into whatever we choose. I have seen the great healing and transformational power that the beautiful and ancient art of yoga holds for people everywhere.

If you have this book in your hands it means you are curious about what yoga may be able to do for you. You may already be practicing at home or be attending public classes. Or perhaps you are a teacher looking for additional information. Either way, you have an idea about the potential for dramatic positive change that yoga holds. This book will give you the information and skills you need to support all levels of personal transformation.

My first two books, Yoga Practice Guides One and Two, share dynamic sequencing for a home practice and for balancing the more subtle energies within the body. To complement them, my Yoga Asana Index illustrates and names (in both Sanskrit and English) nearly all the yoga poses you're likely to come across. While these guides offer a wealth of practice sequences and explanations for their applications, I began to see the need for a book explaining the principles guiding the order and function of each sequence. Readers were also flooding me with requests for a comprehensive guide on postural alignment, a "how to" for the poses themselves.

This book, the Yoga Technique Guide, answers this call by offering a step-by-step system of postural alignment and a clear explanation of effective sequencing. It's like a recipe book for personal practice or class teaching that you can turn to over and over again as you journey on your path of yoga.

When I first began my study of yoga āsana, I had the good fortune of learning from a series of skilled senior teachers. They communicated their detailed knowledge and vast experience with great precision. Still, it was easy to get a little lost sometimes. Each individual pose seemed to have its own complex constellation of alignment cues, which at times I had difficulty absorbing and tracking in my body. While I enjoyed my practice over all, sometimes instead of feeling the delight of embodiment, I found that my practice could get overly cerebral and even tedious. That was my early experience of the individual poses. I wasn't even considering a home practice at that stage. I had no reference for why one pose followed another or where I might be trying to take my practice. It was all pretty mysterious. My experience was probably not unique.

In time, I recognized that understanding the mechanics of each pose and then putting them together in a logical way had the power to positively transform me on a very deep level. My years of apprenticeship in Anusara yoga helped me tremendously in this regard. I eventually earned certification in that style, which gave me a wealth of practical knowledge. Anusara has been the ground from which so much of my practice has flowered. The method was brilliant, but in order to adhere to my own values and pursuit of spiritual growth, and more fully develop my own practice, I moved on. My continuing study of established styles of haṭha yoga, Ayurveda[1], modern biomechanics[2] and even Eastern philosophy, continue to inform and affirm the approach I present in this book.

It is my sincerest hope that this book will be the key to a marvelous personal journey on the path to great health, self-understanding, and sense of unity and completeness within yourself and with the world.

May all beings be happy and free
May my actions and my words contribute
to the happiness and freedom for all.

~ Chant — Lokah, Samastah, Sukhino, Bhavantu

introduction

This book ultimately is about you. It is about your power to positively transform and shape your life. It is about discovering the source of this power within you and how to connect with and maximize it. It is about an entire system designed to help you access this power, with methods you can turn to again and again. It begins with your desire to step more fully into your life and nurture a lasting relationship with your highest potential.

The decision to begin a yoga practice is an exciting first step. Developing an understanding of *how* to practice will usher you toward greater fulfillment. This means learning how to align the body with its highest function and develop an effective progression of yoga postures for specific outcomes. This book serves specifically as a guide to postural alignment and sequencing.

When the body aligns, the spirit soars. Āsana becomes a blessed and sacred dance with each movement coming together as a beautiful, powerful, and harmonious whole. Understanding the principles of sequencing will help individualize your practice and match it with your intention—to soothe you, inspire you, excite you, build your strength, or lull you to sleep. A well-sequenced āsana practice can help center you, open your heart, and connect with your soul.

The first half of this book focuses on alignment, giving you proven alignment principles that apply to any pose. These principles and techniques work to naturally develop stability, optimize strength and flexibility, and foster deep healing.

The second part of the book offers a clear explanation of sequencing to help you create practice sequences for opening and strengthening specific areas of the body. It shares a rationale for why certain poses are often grouped together as well as an explanation of how physical and energetic systems within the body work in yoga.

This book is for yoga practitioners practicing at home or teachers designing classes for students in a studio.

foundations and fundamentals of yoga alignment

about asana practice

getting motivated

Namasté. Everyone who practices yoga is familiar with this short Sanskrit word, which translates as, *"The Light in me sees and acknowledges the same Light in you. We are but one sacred Spirit residing in a myriad of forms."* All approaches to yoga have this united aim: to see the sacred nature in ourselves, in each other, and in all of creation. And then live by that insight. The practice of yoga āsana—along with prāṇāyāma and meditation—is a proven technique for attaining this deeper view.

On a practical, everyday level, āsana practice provides a way for us to meet ourselves where we are, so we can identify changes we wish to make in order to feel better and more free. Yoga āsana helps us more effectively manage our energy. It opens, strengthens, and heals, helping us function at our optimal best.

Getting Motivated

Yoga can be a lifelong commitment to your physical, mental, emotional well-being. It is a lifestyle that encompasses and addresses every aspect of who you are. This is a time-honored technology developed to help each individual optimize his or her life experience. And making that optimization possible requires making your practice a priority, something you stick to. It will be the positive results of your efforts that will keep you coming back to your mat.

There is no single way to develop commitment or a consistent practice. The main thing is to begin. Start with the time you feel you have available in any given day or week. Avoid making grand plans or promises that will be difficult to keep. Instead, start with a realistic first step. Begin with just ten minutes a day!

"Yoga, like brushing teeth, is an acquired preference. When I was young I didn't like brushing my teeth. It required my parents' daily reminding to get me to do it. Now I brush my teeth not only as a prevention against tooth decay but also because I prefer the way my mouth feels when I clean it. The same has been true with my yoga practice. At first it took conscious discipline and deliberate effort to establish a daily practice. Now I practice not only because it's good for me, but because I prefer the way I feel when I do it."

Erich Schiffmann — *Moving Into Stillness*

Practicing at Home or in a Class

For many, learning yoga at a local studio is the best way to learn the details of āsana and develop a feel for the practice. Beautiful and supportive communities often form around studios. Many students find like-minded people who share similar aspirations and values. We feel engaged with others in a unique process of positive self-transformation and growth. We find ourselves among loving, caring friends.

While the class experience is an important and precious one, a personal home practice can have equally profound and transformative benefits. We can take what we learn in class and bring it more deeply into ourselves. Practicing at home can give us the time and space to really feel and explore our movements, breath, and life force. We learn to listen even more acutely to our state of being and act from the knowing that arises. We truly make yoga our own.

In time, we have both our group practice of people joined by the heart and a personal practice reinforcing our individual seat within it.

alignment—why it matters

aligning with the greater whole

Alignment techniques are tools based on sound body mechanics that pragmatically organize movement of the body for optimal integration, stability, and mobility during yoga āsana practice. These principles and techniques are a means to safely and methodically shift limiting patterns and perceptions in the body and help you access yoga postures more deeply.

Alignment techniques are *not* a magic formula for achieving the "perfect" pose. If we hold a fixed concept of an ideal pose or physical form, we are then imposing conformity onto the body. That idea becomes a limitation. Alignment is not a set of rules insisting on conformity but rather a way to guide you toward a deeper sense of self-expression and personal freedom.

Aligning with the Greater Whole

Practicing alignment in yoga poses also invites us to practice a broader form of alignment, fine-tuning our intentions, self-perceptions, self-image, and self-worth, as well as our relationship to others and our environment. We align our highest intentions with our actions so that our actions are a reflection of our aspirations for the highest good for others, the world, and ourselves. We may then align with and embody the qualities of abundant joy, boundless love, compassion, understanding, and forgiveness.

This greater practice of alignment helps us create a sense of integration between our inner world and our outer world. How do we wish to see and experience our relationship to others, our activities, our environment, and even our spiritual connection? What motivates or inspires us? What do we pursue and invite into our lives and what do we move away from or let go? How do we identify and determine what underlies these choices?

While it may not be for everyone, self-observation or self-study is an important facet of yoga practice as a whole. This kind of introspection often impacts our practice of the physical postures. Over time as we begin to heal, strengthen, and refine the flow of energy within our bodies, a ripple effect happens. As we become more sensitive to our physical body, we realize it can offer us direct feedback about our lifestyle choices and general frame of mind. We become more aware of behavior, thoughts, or perceptions that are not for our highest good. For example, you may become more sensitive to how you feel the next day after overindulging at the wine bar on a Saturday night. Or you may no longer feel comfortable with a tendency to judge or criticize others. Or you may find that harboring anger toward someone who hurt you only causes you further pain. Major or minor, this kind of discomfort can inspire us to make new choices that are more in line with our developing sense of self, or the self we wish to become.

"Alignment itself is not the goal. It is a continual dialogue between awareness and action – becoming aware of relationships that exist throughout our body/mind and acting from that awareness. This alignment creates a state of knowing."

~ Bonnie Bainbridge Cohen — *Exploring Body-Mind Centering*

alignment-why it matters

noticing our patterns

Noticing Our Patterns

Each of us has a life history of experiences—joys, sorrows, traumas, and triumphs—held within our body. Every aspect of our physical, mental, and emotional experience is stored in our tissues. These experiences can manifest as habits or patterns of movement in the body that we might not even be aware of. We sometimes interpret these habits and patterns as things our body "just does" or "just can't do." Nearly every physical action we make—standing, walking, running, sitting, raising our arm, breathing—is an ingrained pattern we've established either consciously or unconsciously.

We don't need to judge these patterns as "good" or "bad"—they simply are. But certain ingrained patterns or movements may not be favorable for safe range of motion in the joints, for balance of effort and ease within the muscles, or for overall structural integrity. Additionally, we are looking for optimal energetic flow of the life force known as *Prāṇa.* Our physical alignment directly influences this energetic flow. The practice of the physical postures, or āsana, is a means to positively re-pattern the body, an invitation to create healing and personal freedom.

Practice Is Key

Can yoga āsana be done without any knowledge of alignment? To a limited degree, yes. But understanding alignment technique and developing it in your practice will dramatically increase the effectiveness of your poses and make them more enjoyable.

The techniques offered in this book may be unfamiliar at first and will certainly take a bit of practice. I suggest reading each section and exploring each individual step. Once you have a sense of the individual steps, practice putting them in sequence. Be curious. Play. Finding the appropriate balance in each set of actions may take a little time, and that process will be different for everyone. Sometimes you'll get it right away, sometimes you won't. But with consistent practice, you'll begin to instill each technique in your body and become fluent with it. In time, you'll think less and soar more!

we are energy

the flow of prana

The predominant Western view of the body is as an entity made up of tissues, glands, organs, fluids, and bones. Through yoga, we are invited to take a radically different perspective. Yoga presents the body and mind as an integrated and complex energy system. Everything inside of us is an interplay of subtle energies, ultimately connected to the greater source of Spirit. Our desires, aspirations, and feelings are all interconnected through a subtle flow of energy called *prāṇa*, which means "life force" in the ancient Indian language of Sanskrit. This same energy pervades everything in nature. Yoga, as it is traditionally practiced, concerns itself specifically with how this energy moves through us as human beings and influences all aspects of our being. Yoga considers this prāṇic energy to be a spiritual energy.

The Flow of Prana

Within each pose, alignment helps recruit and direct the internal flow of prāṇa within the body. The conscious movement of our life force not only supports the outer form of the pose from within, but also clears the body, mind, and heart of blocks and facilitates the healing process. Think of a garden hose with water flowing through it. If there are kinks in the hose, the flow of water is hindered. When the hose is realigned and the kinks removed, the water flows optimally. We'll get into more detail on cultivating the flow of prāṇa and yoga āsana in the sections that follow.

After we discuss the principles and techniques of postural alignment, we'll look at an overview of prāṇa in the section, **Prāṇa and Alignment**. We'll see how prāṇa naturally moves in the body and how this relates to the various alignment principles detailed in the book. From this you'll see how the various biomechanical alignment techniques are in fact the means to consciously recruit and direct prāṇa for enhanced power, balance and freedom in your yoga practice.

Basic Form: The Geometry of the Pose

There are essentially nine categories of yoga poses: standing poses, floor poses, forward folds, supine twists, hip openers, seated twists, arm balances, backbends, and inverted poses. Each pose has a distinct shape or geometry that distinguishes it from other poşes and produces unique effects in the body and mind. The most fundamental aspect of alignment is creating the general form of a pose. This includes everything from the direction of the feet to the positioning of the legs and the arms.

The general principles of alignment and action are used the in same way in every yoga pose. They build on one another and are all part of a complete, coherent system. While we may address various areas of the body separately, each alignment principle connects to and integrates with the whole. In other words, what you do in one area affects all other areas.

Refinements

Once you have the basic shape of an individual pose, you begin to refine and deepen the alignment. Within each pose, we work to align the limbs in order to reduce stress in the joints and create optimal stability, integration (strength), freedom (range of motion), overall integrity, balanced muscular action, and prāṇic flow. Without this deeper understanding of detail, a pose can be less effective and may even cause injury. This refinement helps us re-pattern the body and cultivate profound integration and radiant health.

terms and definitions
anatomical neutral

Anatomical Neutral

The concept of *anatomical neutral* is the base reference position for the body. Specific actions initiate from here. Anatomical neutral refers to the position of the feet, legs, and arms when standing. Feet are placed evenly weighted, outer hip width apart, parallel to each other with big toes lined up. Legs are neither rotated out or in but in a “neutral” position with the kneecaps facing forward and vertically aligned with the second toe of the feet. Arms are relaxed at the sides with the palms facing in toward the body.

The Back Plane of the Body

This term, *back plane of the body,* refers to the *posterior* aspect of the body. It is often used to indicate a general directionality of movement. In a standing pose such as Tāḍāsana (Mountain pose), both the top of the femur (leg bone) and the top of the humerus (arm bone) should move toward the back plane of the body. This action sets the limbs deeper in the socket of the hip and shoulder. It creates more integration and stability in these major joints and is part of *Muscular Engagement.*

Core Midlines

Two main lines or axes divide the body. One is a *vertical midline*, which divides the body into right and left halves through the center. The other is a *horizontal midline* dividing the upper body from the lower body at the top pelvis. Both are significant centers into and out of which energy in the body flows.

Summary*: Energy moves into and out of the core lines of the body.*

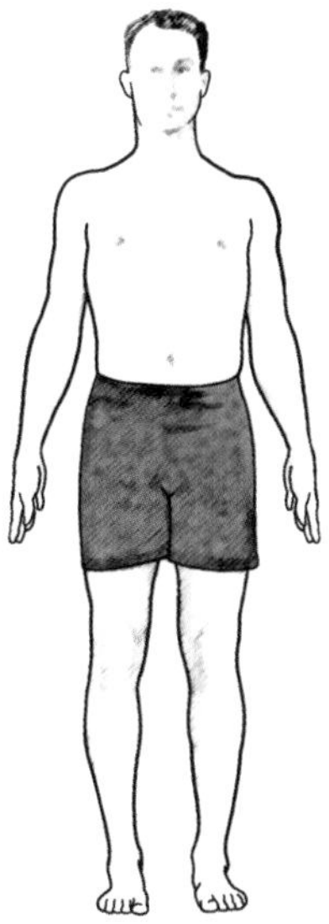

Anatomical Neutral is the position of the body from which movement is initiated.

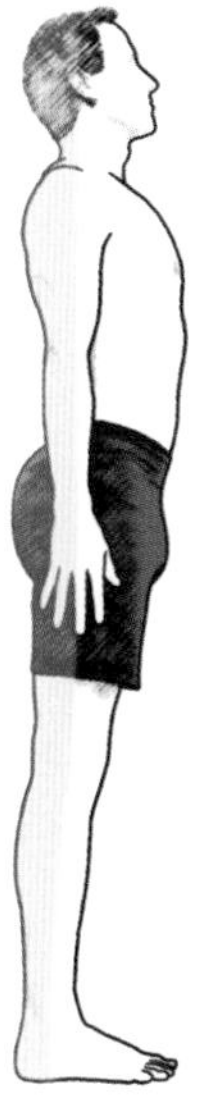

The Back Plane of the Body refers to the posterior aspect of the body.

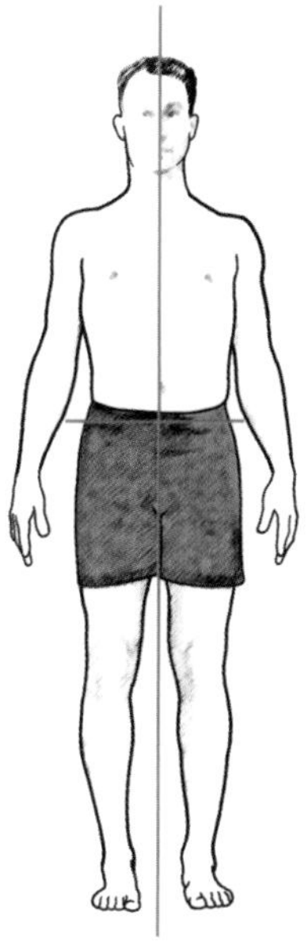

Core Midlines are axes that divide the body.

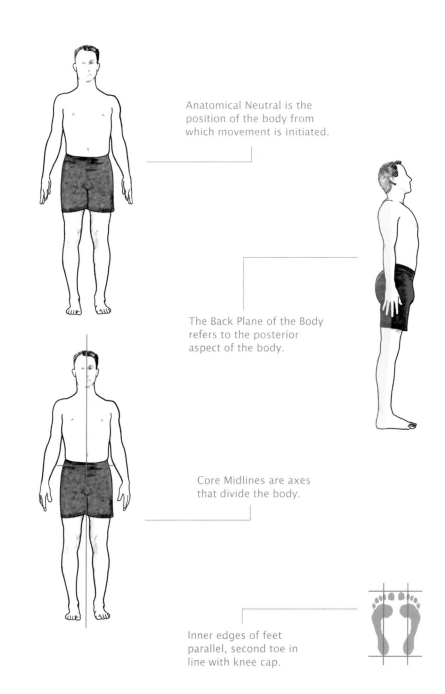

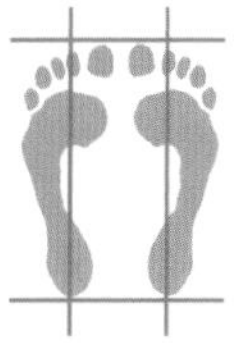

Inner edges of feet parallel, second toe in line with knee cap.

terms and definitions
muscular engagement

Muscular Engagement

Muscular Engagement refers to the intentional, coordinated engagement of muscles in the body during āsana. This action can be described as "hugging" the muscles to the bones on all sides and integrating the limbs and joints to create more stability. Muscular Engagement moves from the outside inward, toward the core lines of the body. It draws the limbs toward the midline of the body. This engagement draws from the *foundation* of the pose—that part of the body in contact with the earth, whether directly or indirectly through a prop—into the core midlines of the body. This conscious engagement creates overall physical integration, strength, and stability in a pose. It draws the various parts of the outer body closer together. By initiating Muscular Engagement, we create more awareness and sensitivity. Muscular Engagement is initiated by and is reflective of the strength of our intentions, desires, and will.

Summary: Muscular Engagement *is a conscious, coordinated engagement of the muscles onto the bones on all sides and an integrating of the limbs and joints to create more stability. Muscular Engagement moves from the outside inward, toward the core lines of the body.*

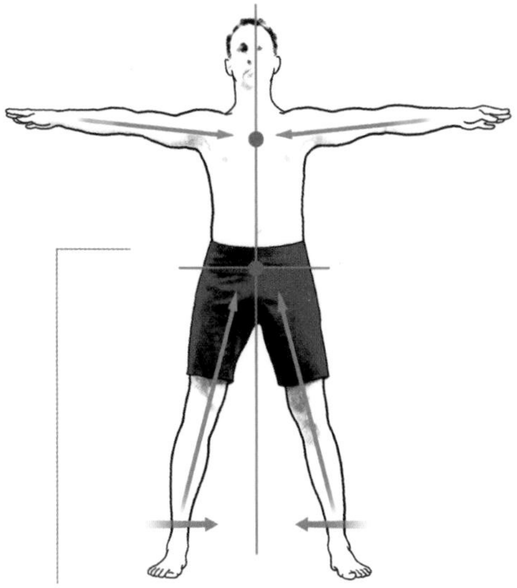

Muscular Engagement moves from the outside inward, toward the core lines of the body.

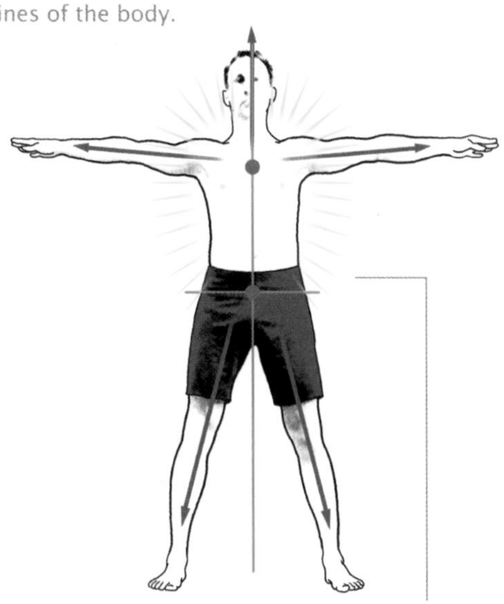

Energetic Extension moves outwards from the core through the core lines of the body.

Energetic Extension

Energetic Extension refers to the intentional reaching or lengthening of the limbs and spine in any yoga pose. It follows Muscular Engagement, which sets a stable stage from which to expand outwards. In the limbs it is used to expand and extend energy outwards from the core through the core lines of the body. In the spine it is the conscious lengthening up from the pelvis to the crown of the head. It is the powerful expanding, lengthening, and widening energy that radiates out in all directions. Energetic Extension is expressive: it lengthens the limbs, opens the joints, and widens the limbs away from each other and away from the core.

Summary: Energetic Extension *always follows* Muscular Engagement. *It expands and extends outwards from the core through the core lines of the body and limbs. It is a powerfully expanding, lengthening, and widening energy that radiates out in all directions.*

Note: *The balance of Muscular Engagement and Energetic Extension invites a deeper, stronger, more intrinsic energy that brings lightness, expansion, and freedom of movement to your poses. These two complementary energies are always more powerful than mere muscular contraction alone. Muscular Engagement is always initiated first, followed by Energetic Extension. Both should be maintained in balance throughout a posture or flow of postures.*

foundations of the pose

feet and hands as foundation

Feet and Hands as Foundation

In many poses, the feet and hands are the foundation of the pose. In primary contact with the floor, they support the rest of the body. How we set the foundation has a distinct influence on the dynamic of any pose and will affect everything above it.

Four Corners of the Foot

It can be useful to think of the feet as having "four corners" to help us stand firmly in any pose. These four corners are:
1) Outer mound of the big toe
2) Inner edge of the heel
3) Mound of the little toe
4) Outer edge of the heel

In every standing pose, all four corners of the foot should work evenly by pressing into the floor.

1. Start by first spreading out your toes.
2. Anchor the mound of your big toe down.
3. Keep that and draw back to the inner edge of your heel.
4. Anchor that inner edge, then draw across from your big toe mound to your little toe mound, anchoring that.
5. Lastly, draw from your little toe mound back to the outer edge of your heel.

Try this sequence of actions on one foot and compare it to the other foot. Notice how when you mindfully place the foot in this way it will feel distinctly different than the other foot. You may even notice the entire leg feels different, even right up through the whole side of the body. It may feel a little more solid, lighter, more extended or expansive. Like the legs, the feet also use Muscular Engagement and Energetic Extension simultaneously. In fact the actions of the feet initiate the ability to create Muscular Engagement of the legs! The actions of the feet engage the front and sides of your shin as well as the calf.

Play around with mindfully placing the feet in this way. After a while, setting your foundation will become second nature.

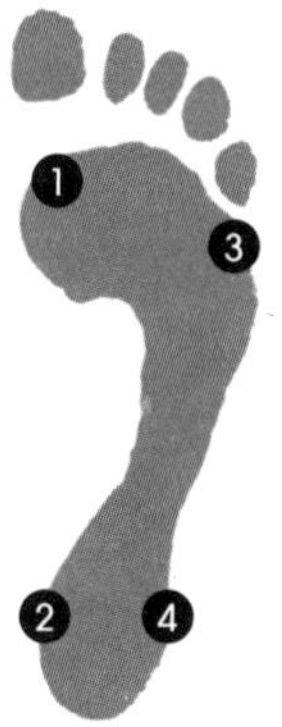

For standing poses, all four corners of the foot should work evenly by pressing into the floor.
1. Outer mound of the big toe
2. Inner edge of the heel
3. Mound of the little toe
4. Outer edge of the heel

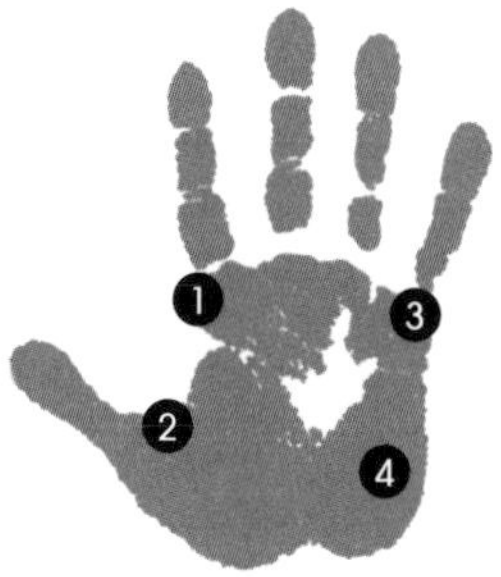

When the hands are part of the foundation the Four Corners ground evenly and are:
1. Base of the index finger
2. Base of the thumb
3. Base of the little finger
4. Heel of the hand on the little finger side

Four Corners of the Hand

The four corners describe the placement of the hand when part of the foundation such as in Adho-Mukha Śvanāsana (Downward Facing Dog pose).

The four corners of the hand are:
1) Base of the index finger.
2) Base of the thumb
3) Base of the little finger
4) Heel of the hand on the little finger side

In any pose with hands flat on the floor, all four corners of the hands should press down. Also, with fingers spread, the whole length of each finger should also be pressed firmly into the floor.

With these actions of the hands, see if you can notice a toning and lifting effect on the center of your palms. When you activate your hands in this way the energy of the center of the palm draws up your arms toward the core of your body creating a deeper sense of integration. It is part of initiating Muscular Engagement in the arms.

***Summary**: In every standing pose, ground down the four corners of your feet in this order: big toe mound, inner edge of the heel, little toe mound then outer edge of the heel. In your hands, press into the floor the base of the index finger, the base of the thumb, the base of the little finger, and the heel of the hand on the little finger side.*

***Note**: Pay particular attention to the grounding of the inside corners of your hand—the base of your index finger and the base of your thumb—as they have a tendency to unconsciously lift from the floor.*

basic form

the feet in standing poses

The Feet in Standing Poses

A solid foundation will influence the form, balance, strength, and openness in standing poses. The two main types of standing poses are front-facing poses and lateral or side-facing poses.

In front-facing poses, where one foot is forward of the other such as in Vīrabhadrāsana I (Warrior I), your front foot points straight forward with your second toe in line with the center of your shin and knee. Your back foot is placed at a 45-degree angle. Your front and back heels line up or the rear foot can be even slightly wider, to let your inner thigh rotate inward more effectively. This helps your hips to find an even, front-facing position. Plant all four corners of your feet evenly.

For lateral-facing poses such as Vīrabhadrāsana II (Warrior II), line up your front foot with the center of your front shin and knee. Place your rear foot at a right angle to the front foot, and parallel to the back edge of the mat. Line up the arch of your rear foot with the center of the heel of your front foot. Having the rear foot at a 90-degree angle in relation to the front foot can allow for more balanced inward rotation of the rear leg. When the actions of the rear leg are in balance, the pelvis can then face open to the side evenly with no twist or torque in the hips.

***Summary**: In front-facing poses, front foot points straight forward. Second toe in line with the center of your shin and knee. Back foot is placed at a 45-degree angle. Front and back heels line up or rear foot can be slightly wider. In lateral-facing poses, line up front foot with the center of front shin and knee. Place rear foot at a right angle to front foot, or parallel to the back edge of the mat. Remember, how you set the foundation affects everything above it.*

Foot position in front facing poses

(Rear foot can also be placed wider)

Foot position in lateral or side facing poses

Vīrabhadrāsana I (Warrior I)
(front facing pose)

Vīrabhadrāsana II (Warrior II)
(lateral facing pose)

alignment principles
the legs and pelvis

The Legs and Pelvis

To explain the principles of leg and pelvis alignment, we'll look at Tāḍāsana (Mountain pose). In this pose, two sets of complementary actions align the legs and pelvis. They are done in sequence. The first set of actions should be maintained while the second sets of actions are implemented, without overpowering the first. The goal is to maintain the two sequential sets of actions in balance and harmony.

First: **Legs**

1. Establish the foundation of the pose by working the principles of the feet and set the four corners.
2. Engage the muscles of your legs (Muscular Engagement).
3. With Muscular Engagement maintained, actively press your inner legs toward each other (in toward the vertical midline) from your feet right up to the upper most part of your inner thighs.
4. Check with your hands to ensure that the upper, inner thighs, just below the floor of your pelvis, are firmly engaged.
5. Maintaining firm Muscular Engagement of your legs as a whole, rotate or "turn" the upper, inner thighs back and apart.

The initial effect of these first actions sets your thigh bones back toward the back plane of the body while deepening and softening your groin. This also has the affect of widening your upper, inner thighs away from the vertical midline and each other. The crest of your pelvis tilts forward and your belly softens. It also moves your sit bones back and apart and tilts the top of your sacrum forward and broadens the floor of the pelvis.

Next: **Pelvis**

1. Maintain the first set of actions described above.
2. Lengthen your tailbone down and slightly under and draw up and in from your pubic bone toward your navel. This set of actions, combined with the first set, subtly domes the floor of your pelvis upward and tones your lower abdomen.

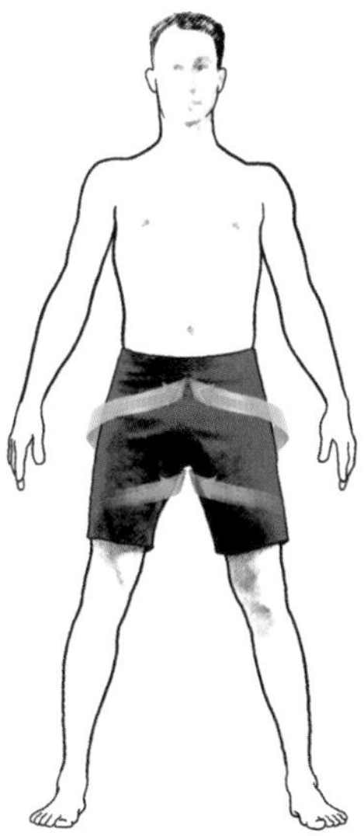

Inner rotation of the legs

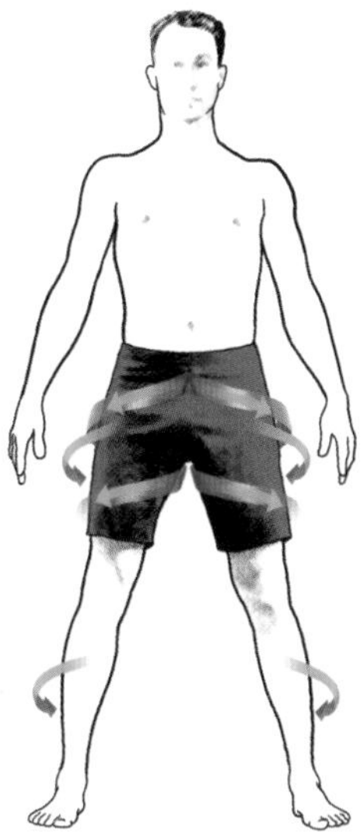

Outer rotation of the legs

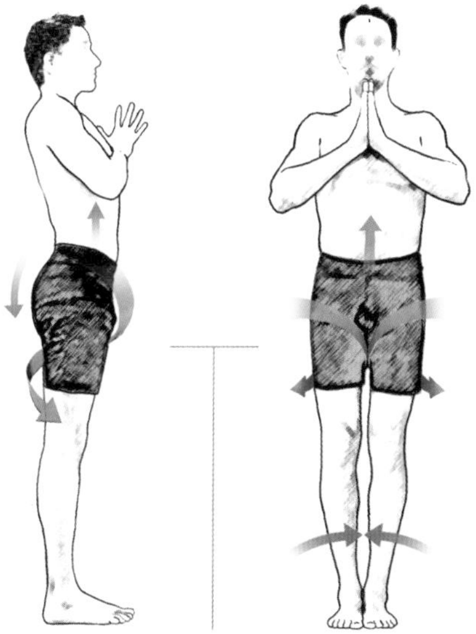

Balanced actions of the legs and pelvis

3. With both sets of actions maintained in balanced combination, set the top of your thigh bone deeply in the hip socket and draw energy up from the tailbone, or "the root of the spine." This stabilizing and ascending energy current moves up through the central axis of the body, in front of the spine and behind the navel, creating a column of support within the waist for the upper body.

Note: *These actions create what is known as* Mūla Bandha *and* Uḍḍīyāna Bandha *and are used in every pose to some degree (see Bandhas on page 34). These two bandhas connect the power and stability of the lower limbs through the area of the pelvis, thus generating extension, expansion, and freedom in the upper body. Mūla Bandha and Uḍḍīyāna Bandha become the juncture, or the actions that join the power, strength and stability of the lower body to create an ascending, expanding energy in the upper body. The combined work of these two bandhas supports, lengthens, and enhances the flexibility of your spine as well as your chest, shoulders and neck. They create a platform from which your upper body and limbs derive power and extension.*

alignment principles
the legs and pelvis

***Summary**:*

Alignment of Legs and Pelvis

1. *Place the four corners of the feet onto the floor.*
2. *Muscular Engagement of the legs. Press your legs toward the vertical midline.*
3. *Rotate your upper inner thighs back and apart.*
4. *Sit bones lift and broaden. Top of the sacrum tilts forward. Floor of the pelvis broadens.*
5. *Lengthen tailbone down.*
6. *Pubic bone lifts. Floor of the pelvis draws up. Lower abdomen firms and draws in and up.*

Here's How to Practice This

Try this sequence of movements. It will really help you to get an understanding of the various alignment actions of the legs and pelvis. We'll break each individual movement down so you can get a tangible experience in your body. We'll then bring them together step by step until all the principles are working in concert.

Individual Excercises

1. Cow/Cat with a block high up between the thighs.
2. Standing Cow/Cat with block.
3. Standing with a block between the shins, press in toward the vertical midline.
4. Belt the thighs, rotate the upper inner thighs back and apart, pressing the thighs out into the belt.

Put It All Together

1. In standing, bend the kness slightly to initiate Muscular Engagement.
2. Isometrically press the shins to the vertical midline.
3. Keep that, rotate the upper, inner thighs back and apart.
4. Tailbone down, pubic bone and and lower belly lift, side of the waist back.

Cow/Cat with Block

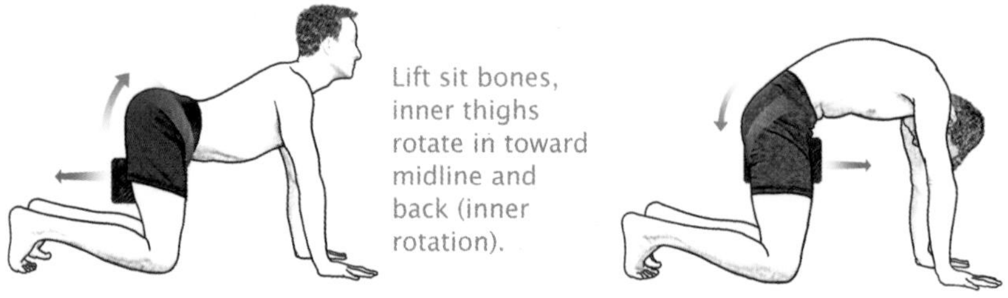

Lift sit bones, inner thighs rotate in toward midline and back (inner rotation).

Tuck tailbone, inner thighs rotate forward and and out away from midline (outer rotation).

Standing Cow/Cat

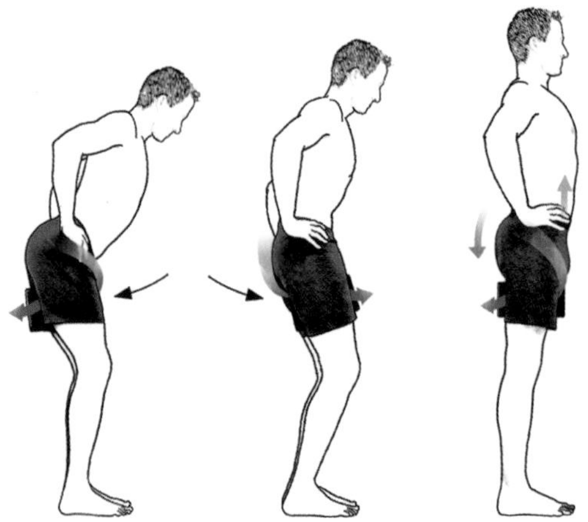

Move back and forth between Cow and Cat. Finish by balancing Cow with Cat (inner/outer rotation).

Block and Strap

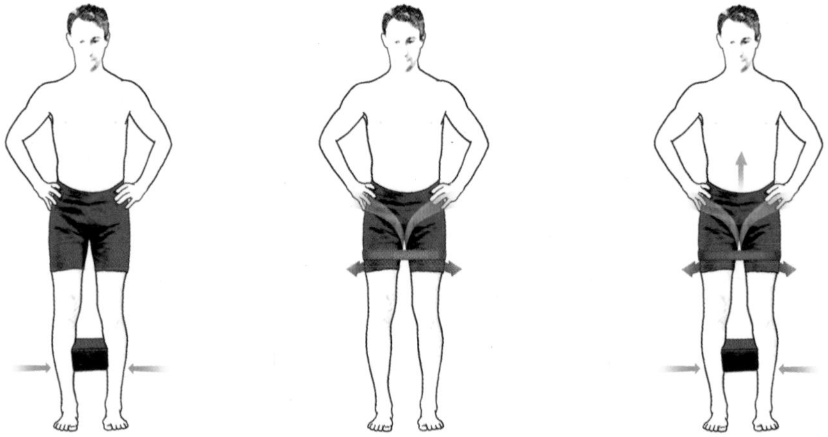

Squeeze a block between the shins, engaging the upper inner thighs.

Rotate inner thighs back and apart pressing out into belt.

Balance actions. Squeeze block, then rotate inner thighs back pressing into belt.

alignment principles
ankles and knees

Ankles and Knees

There are two common patterns in the feet and ankles that can be problematic. *Pronation* is a dropping of the aches and a falling in of the ankles toward the midline. *Supination* is when the weight of the foot falls toward the outer edge causing the ankles to bow away from the midline.

Both these habitual patterns create an imbalance in the foundation and stress on the joints. These patterns are addressed by the above-mentioned principles of the feet and legs. Establishing the four corners activates the muscles that support the feet and ankles, allowing weight in the feet to be distributed more evenly. The work in the legs helps rebalance the position of the ankles and lower legs.

As with the ankles and shins, our knees can also either drop in toward each other ("knock knees") or bow away from each other ("bow legs"). Often these actions follow the tendencies of the ankles, pronating or supinating.

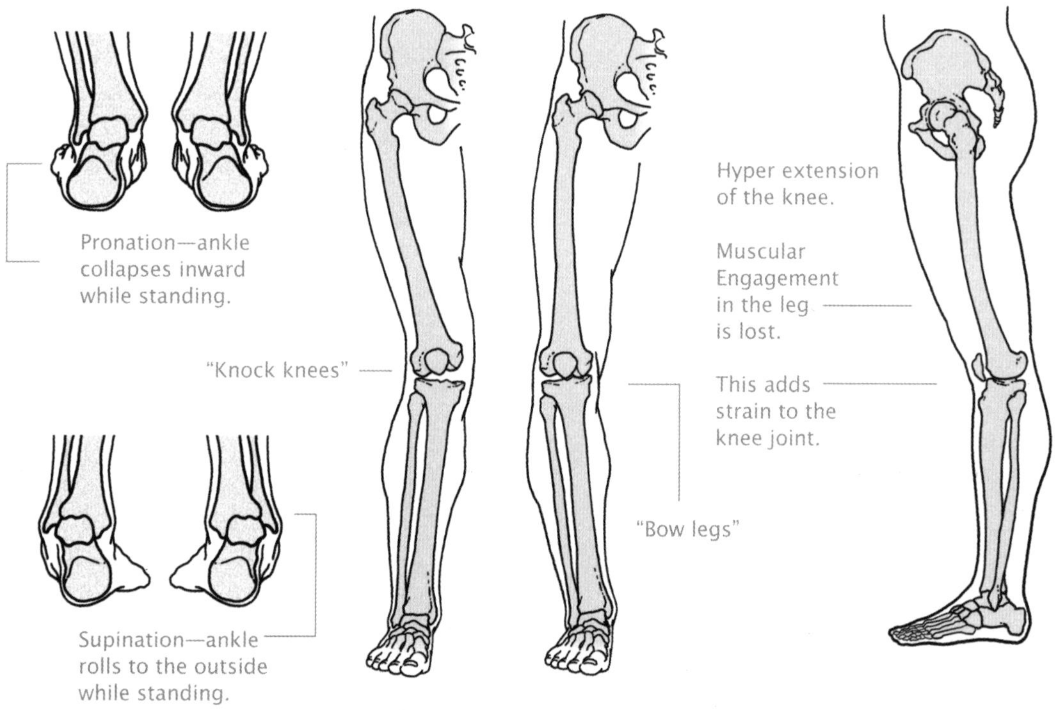
Pronation—ankle collapses inward while standing.
"Knock knees"
Supination—ankle rolls to the outside while standing.
"Bow legs"
Hyper extension of the knee.
Muscular Engagement in the leg is lost.
This adds strain to the knee joint.

Addressing Pronation
To re-pattern pronation, put special focus on the outer two corners of your feet. Maintain firm Muscular Engagement in your legs and emphasize the widening apart of your upper thigh bones. This will help your lower legs stay firm and in balance with the midline.

Addressing Supination
To re-pattern supination, put special focus on the inner edges of your feet. Maintain consistent Muscular Engagement and firm commitment to the vertical midline in your lower legs to keep your ankles and shins from bowing away from each other.

Hyperextension of the Knee
Hyperextension of the knee is when the knee bends past straight toward the back of the knee joint. When the joint moves to this position, the muscles of the thigh will shut off and Muscular Engagement in the leg is lost. This adds strain to the knee joint as well as significantly diminishing prāṇic flow through the leg and the rest of the body.

To address this pattern, strong muscular work in the legs is required:
1. Firmly establish the four corners of your feet.
2. Bend your knee slightly to initiate Muscular Engagement in your thighs.
3. Press your toes firmly down and isometrically[3] draw your foot back. This draws the base of your shin back at the ankle and fires up your calf muscles and hamstrings.
4. From the foundation of your foot, draw up your leg with Muscular Engagement toward your hip, essentially pulling your leg straighter from the ground up.
5. Keep all of that work and press out from your hip down through your leg to the foundation. Maintain the Muscular Engagement of your thigh, calf, and hamstrings.

Lower Back

The shape of the lower back is determined by both how the feet are placed and the position of the legs and pelvis. There are two common postural patterns in a standing position that create either a deep curve in or a flattening of the lower back.

An overly curved lower back is called *Lordosis* (Fig. 2) and is caused by one of two things. Either the top of the thighs and hips push forward and cause the chest and shoulders to sink (we see clothing models do this a lot!), or the top thighs press back lifting the buttocks and causing the top of the sacrum to tilt forward. In either case, the result is an overarching of the lumbar spine, which creates compression in the lower back.

The second common pattern creates a flattening of the lower back, called *Kyphosis* (Figs. 3-4). This comes from the legs outwardly rotating and the top of the thighs push forward. The pelvis pushes forward and the sacrum tilts back along with the lumbar spine. This position of the legs and hips creates a dropping and sinking of the chest and shoulders.

A flattening of the lower back is also present in what is often termed as a "military" posture (Fig. 3). This is when the tailbone and sacrum are forcefully tucked under, flattening the lumbar curve in the lower back. The thoracic curve of the upper back is rigid and flattened to forcefully lift the chest. The chin is drawn back toward the throat and the back of the head is strongly lengthened up, creating a flattening of the cervical spine of the neck.

Again, how our lower backs behave in a pose will be determined by how we set our foundation and how we work our legs and pelvis. The key is always to create balanced action in the lower body.

1. With the feet outer hip width apart, establish the four corners of the feet.
2. Bend the knees slightly to increase Muscular Engagement.
3. Place and keep a hand on the lower back to monitor the lumbar curve.
4. Isometrically squeeze the shins toward each other.
5. Keeping the knees slightly bent, turn the upper, inner thighs back and apart, deepening the groins.
6. Notice how the lumbar curve becomes more pronounced or "deepens."
7. Lengthen the tailbone down, without overpowering the actions of the upper thighs.
8. Keep the balance of actions between the thighs and the tailbone and straighten the legs.

***Note**: When you are changing any habitual pattern, in this case how you stand, the change may at first feel unnatural and exaggerated. With some practice the new alignment will become the new norm.*

Fig 1 Fig 2 Fig 3 Fig 4

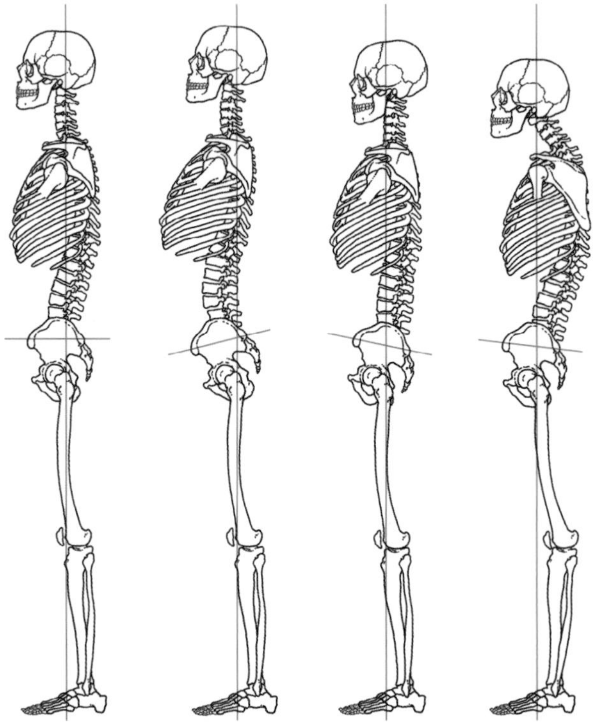

Fig 1 - Balanced
Fig 2 - Lordotic—overly curved lower back
Fig 3 - Kyphotic—Flat lower back, flat upper back, flat neck
Fig 4 - Kyphotic—Flat lower back, knees hyper extended, shoulders rolled forward, sunken chest, extend flat neck

Shoulders

How we consciously place our shoulders and shoulder blades affects the mobility of our upper back, chest, and neck. Many of us tend to slouch, rounding our shoulders and dropping them forward. This puts strain on our neck, sinks our chest, and decreases strength and flexibility in our upper back. This rounding happens because our shoulder blades slide forward away from our spine. When our shoulders droop forward, it also causes a loss of "fullness" or lift in our torso, a reflection of diminished prāṇic flow. In addition, this posture diminishes our breathing capacity.

The whole unit of the arm and shoulder are jointed to the torso through the collarbone at the sternoclavicular joint, the place where the collarbone connects to the sternum at the base of the throat. This means that the entire shoulder blade has quite a range of motion around the back and sides of the ribcage.

Aligning the Shoulders

Use breath and these actions to create alignment in the shoulders:

1. First create stability in the foundation of your lower body (legs and pelvis). Draw your breath in from that firm platform.
2. With the inhale, fill your whole torso from the "bottom" up. Envision a glass being filled with water, or a room being filled with an ever-brightening light.
3. Supported by this inner radiance, soften your shoulders then consciously raise them up from your hips through the sides of your torso. Avoid pulling them up by the muscles at the base of your neck. Maintain this inner lift.
4. Next bring the top of your shoulders and upper arms back toward the back plane of the body. Slide your shoulder blades back and hug the inner edges toward each other (but avoid squeezing them together!).
5. With a fullness in the back body, bring the lower tips of your shoulder blades forward through the bottom of your heart and diaphragm, then up toward your chest. This supports a steady lift in your chest and openness across your collar-bones and throat. Even your upper palate slides back and feels open.

Try This

I call this gesture, "how wonderful." It helps to really get a sense of the actions of the shoulders and of the lower ends of the shoulder blades moving forward and lifting the chest.

1. On an inhale, create an inner fullness of the torso.
2. Raise your ams out to the side, elbows slightly bent, palms up.
3. Move the tops of the shoulders back. Turn your palms to face more behind you. Thumbs begin to point down. This rotates the whole upper arm.
4. Feel the lower tips of the shoulder blades moving inward toward the heart. The chest will expand and rise.
5. Keep all the actions of the shoulders and lower the arms back down.

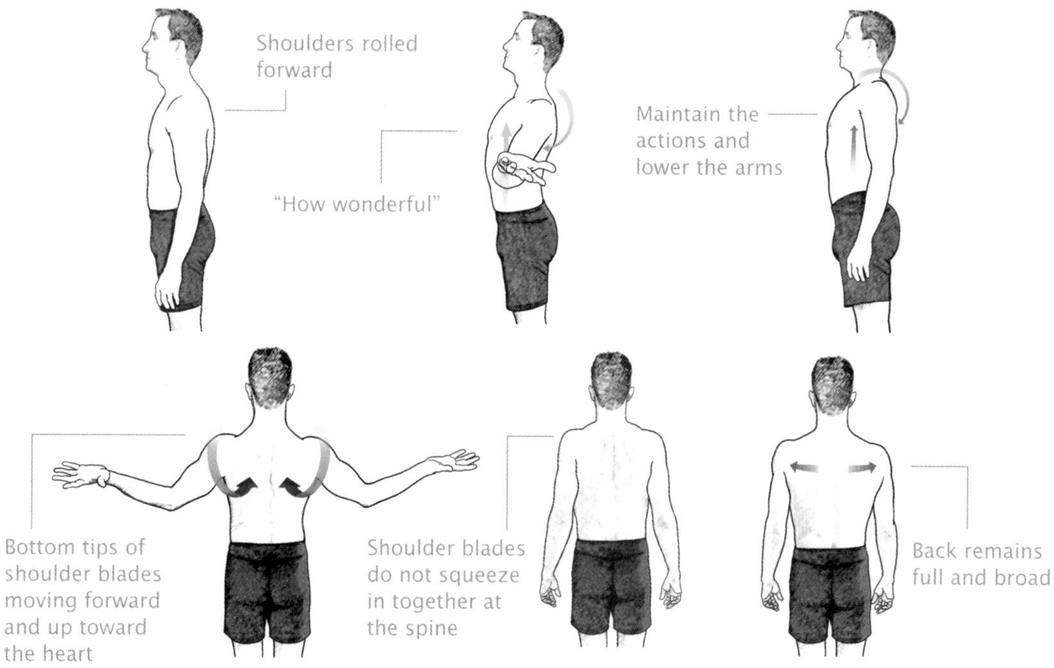
Shoulders rolled forward
"How wonderful"
Maintain the actions and lower the arms
Bottom tips of shoulder blades moving forward and up toward the heart
Shoulder blades do not squeeze in together at the spine
Back remains full and broad

***Note**: If the above actions have caused you to jut your lower ribs forward and over arch your lower back, renew the lengthening of your tailbone and draw your lower ribs gently back toward the back plane of your body.*

alignment principles

alignment of the arms

Alignment of the Arms

Our arms have considerable range of motion. This is due to the relatively shallow ball and socket joint of the shoulder as well as the mobility of the shoulder blade on the back of the ribcage. The principles of alignment for arms are the same for all poses, yet the position of the hand will differ depending on the pose. The key actions include rotating the upper arm slightly outward, then actively moving the upper arm toward the back plane of the body. This sets the head of the arm bone into the shoulder socket using the principle of Muscular Engagement. These actions are maintained whether the arm is in movement or in a static or fixed position. Depending on the pose, the forearm and hand will turn independent of the action of the upper arm.

Alignment of the arms is initiated first by the actions of the shoulders. We'll use Tāḍāsana as the example pose.

1. Using the breath, establish an inner fullness and length in the torso.
2. Maintaining the expansiveness of the torso, move the shoulder blades toward the back plane of the body.
3. The upper arm bones draw back and rotate outward (this will initially turn the palms open).
4. The arms now can be moved in any direction. The first three actions remain constant.
5. The actions of the upper arm and shoulder are the same no matter which way the forearms and palms are turned.

***Note**: In any pose, the shoulder blades move onto the back and toward the spine (vertical midline) but do not squeeze together. The back remains full and broad.*

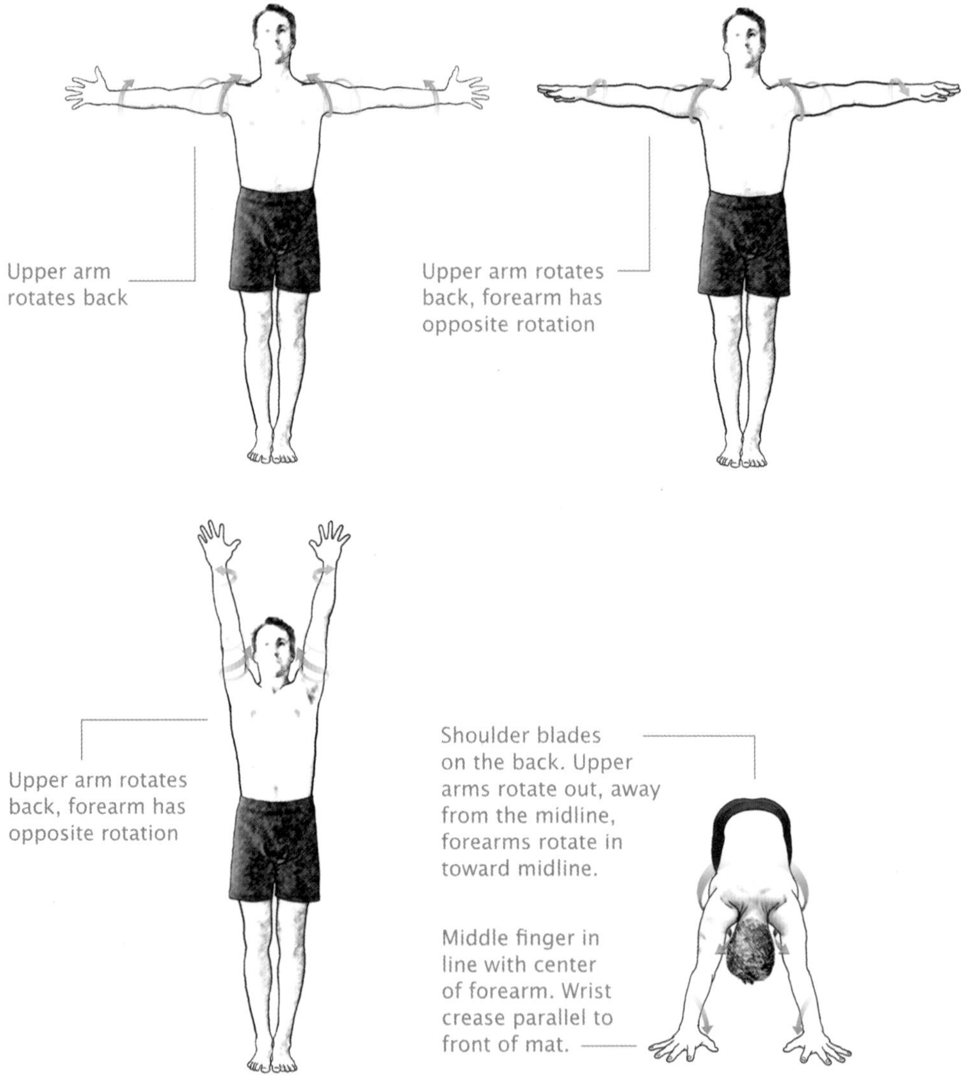
Upper arm rotates back
Upper arm rotates back, forearm has opposite rotation
Upper arm rotates back, forearm has opposite rotation
Shoulder blades on the back. Upper arms rotate out, away from the midline, forearms rotate in toward midline.
Middle finger in line with center of forearm. Wrist crease parallel to front of mat.

In Adho-Mukha Śvanāsana (Downward Facing Dog pose), upper arms rotate up away from the floor and away from the midline. Forearms rotate in opposite direction from elbow to base of thumb. (Same as with arms overhead when standing). Create balance between drawing the outer edges of the shoulder blades away from the floor toward the back plane of the body, and rotating the upper arm outward away from the midline.

Moving the Arms

When positioning the arms in āsana practice, the head of the arm bone is first integrated into the shoulder socket using the principle of Muscular Engagement. This means that from the fingers through the length of the arm, there is firming of the muscles onto the bones of the arm and shoulder and a drawing in toward the center, or core, of the torso. Once the shoulder is "set" in this way the arm is then fully extended using the principle of Energetic Extension. With these two principles maintained in balance, the arms can be moved in any direction. Movement is initiated first from the core of the body out.

We'll first use the example of the upper arm in Utthita Trikoṇāsana (Extended Triangle pose).

1. Straighten your arm up and somewhat forward of your shoulder.
2. Spread the fingers to initiate Muscular Engagement.
3. Lengthen the sides of the body.
4. Firm all the muscles of the arm onto the bone.
5. Draw from the fingers through the length of the arm in toward the shoulder and the core of the body (Vertical Midline).
6. Keeping that engagement, reach back out from the core to the fingers (Energetic Extension).
7. Turn from the core and shoulder to open the arm.

In a bound twist, the arms are moved into position for a static bind, yet the principles still apply in the same way. We'll use Ardha Matsyendrāsana I (Half Matsyendra's pose) as an example.

1. Bring your elbow over your knee.
2. Lengthen the sides of the body.
3. Bring the shoulders up and back with Muscular Engagement.
4. Then initiate your turn keeping the torso long, the chest full and shoulders up and back.
5. Maintain these actions and bind the hands.

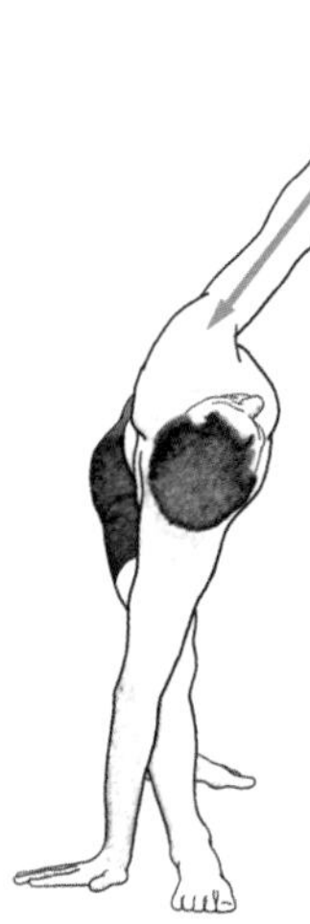

Engage and draw into the core.

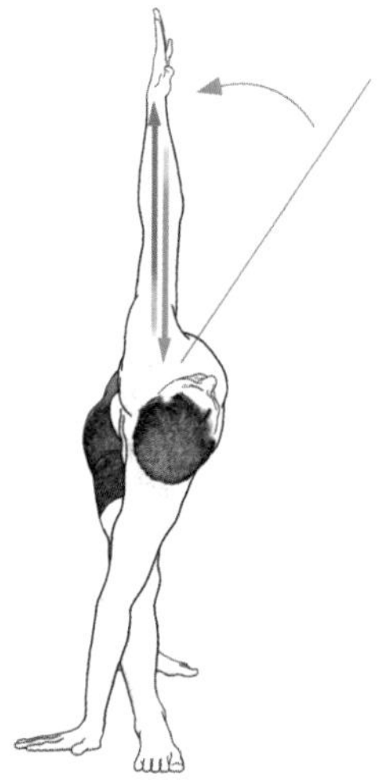

Staying connected to the core, expand out and turn open from the core of the torso.

A common misalignment is to move the arm open from the hand before integrating. This puts strain on the shoulder joint. ⊘

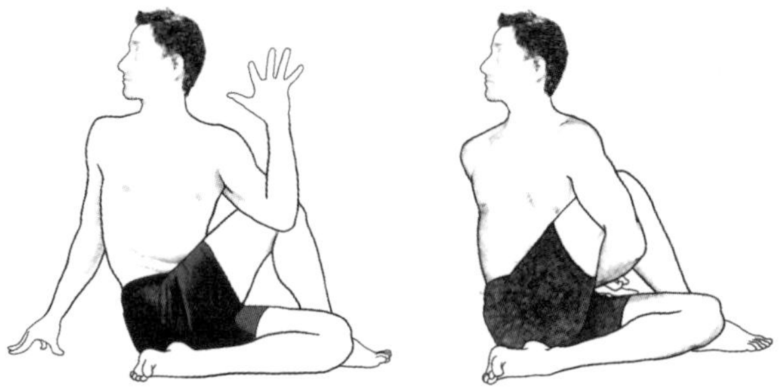

With balanced action, turn open from the core of the torso with the chest full and the shoulders up and back.

A common misalignment is to let the bind shorten the torso and bring the shoulder forward and down. ⊘

alignment principles
head and neck

Head and Neck

For healthy alignment in yoga, we are looking to cultivate a neutral position of the head and an unrestricted, lengthened natural curve in the neck. One common pattern is to jut the chin forward, bringing the head more to the front plane of the body. This puts an increased load on the muscles of the neck and shoulders, creates an overly deep curve in the vertebrae of the neck, and causes compression at the top of the cervical spine.

Another habit is just the opposite: drawing the chin back toward the throat. This creates too much length in the neck and the back of the skull, flattening the cervical spine, which causes tightness in the throat and jaw, and tension in the sides and back of the neck. This often is termed “military posture:” chest strongly lifted with the neck and upper back flat.

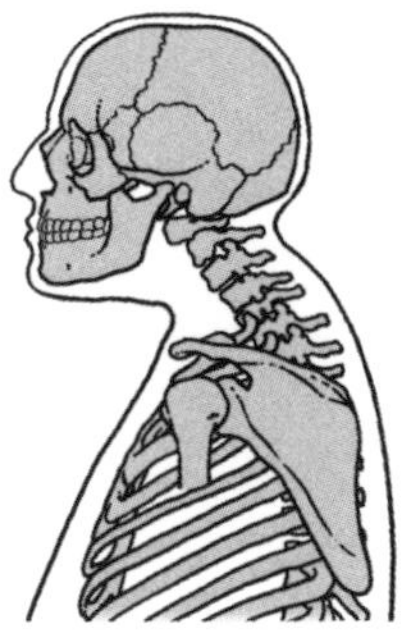

Chin extends out, removing the curve and flattening the neck.

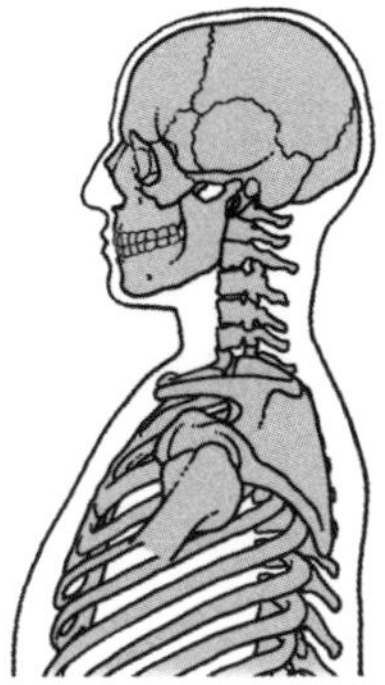

Chin pulls in, also removing the curve and flattening the neck.

Actions for the Neck

In a standing position, to bring your neck into its natural curve and your head into a more neutral position:

1. First set your shoulders following the guidelines for shoulders (see page 23).
2. Draw the sides of your throat, from the base to just below the hinge of the jaw, towards the back plane.
3. Slide your upper palate back. This helps your chin tilt up and your head tilt slightly back and brings a gentle curve to your cervical spine.
4. Keep this and lengthen up the back of your skull, bringing your eyes and chin back to a level position without losing the curve in your neck.

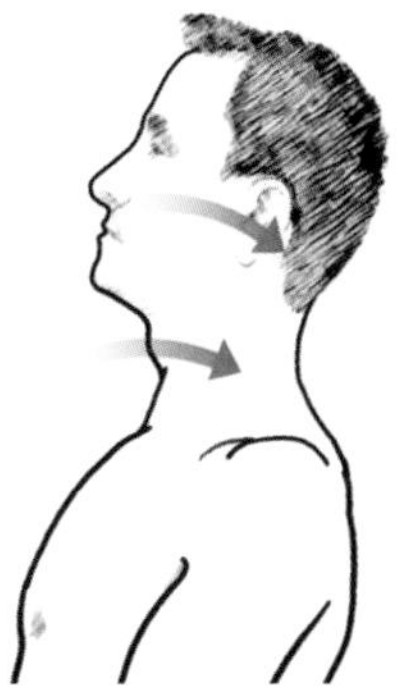

Sides of the throat draw back. Top of the palette back.

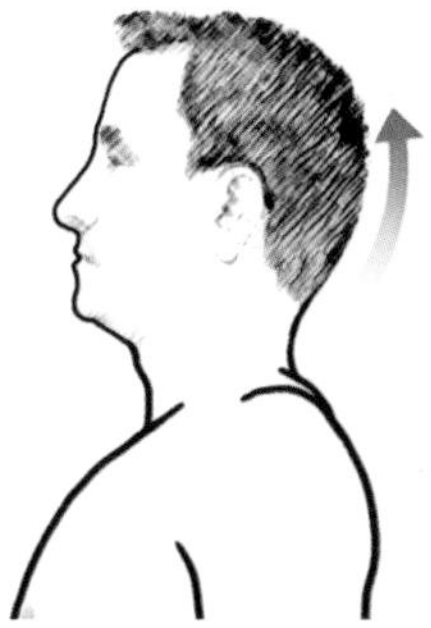

Maintain first actions, lengthen back of the skull upward.

When the head is turned
When the head is turned to the right or left, the alignment is the same. Basically maintain the inner lift of your torso, align your shoulders without hardening your upper back, bring your neck and head into the neutral position as described above, *then turn the head.*

When looking up or in back bends
In a backbend such as Dhanurāsana (Bow pose), many people tend to push their throat and chin forward and collapse at the back of their neck just below the base of the skull. When looking up in poses such as Bhujaṅgāsana (Cobra pose) or Tāḍāsana (Mountain pose) with arms raised, the main thing to be aware of is that your head will be tilted farther back with an increased curve in the cervical spine. Align as you would for a standing position and as you look up, emphasize the drawing back of the sides of your throat below the hinge of the jaw while lengthening the back of your skull upward. This helps prevent compression where the cervical spine meets the skull.

***Summary**: First align the shoulders. The sides of the throat and palette move toward the back plane. Tilt the head back to create a gentle curve in the cervical spine. Add slight length to the back of the skull, bringing the eyes and chin back to level. Do this while maintaining the curve in the neck.*

more about feet and hands

when not the foundation

Feet — When Not the Foundation

The feet play an important role in creating integration, stability, and extension in the legs even when they are not part of the foundation. The actions of the feet in non-standing poses are basically the same as when you are standing on the ground. The important thing is to create balanced action in the feet and lower leg. Two additional actions can help you create that balance.

Try this sitting on the floor with one leg extended straight:

1. First spread your toes and draw them back toward your knee. Reach out through your heel as you do this. Notice that pulling your toes toward you activates the muscles on the top of your foot and front of your shin. The extended heel lengthens the arch of your foot and the back of the calf.
2. Hold this for a moment and then relax.
3. Next point your toes and foot away from you. This activates the arch and engages the calf muscles and also lengthens the top of the foot and front of the shin. Hold this for a moment and then relax.
4. To create balanced action, do both of these things together. First spread your toes and flex your ankle, reaching out through your heel.
5. Maintain that and press out and forward through the ball of your foot. With these two actions combined, your entire foot and lower part of your leg are both muscularly engaged and extended at the same time.
6. Keep the bottom of your foot even (remember the four corners), not turned inward. Press through the ball of your foot to prevent this potential turning of the ankle. The balance of Muscular Engagement and Energetic Extension integrates the limbs into the core of the body while creating radiant extension back out from the core.

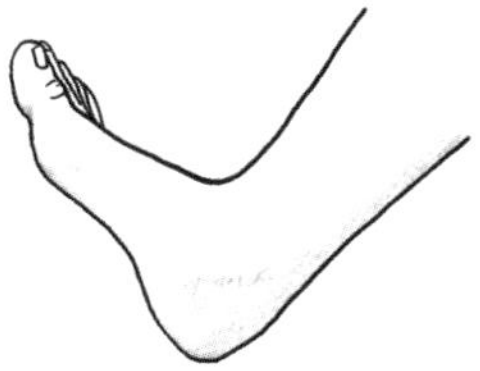

Flexed

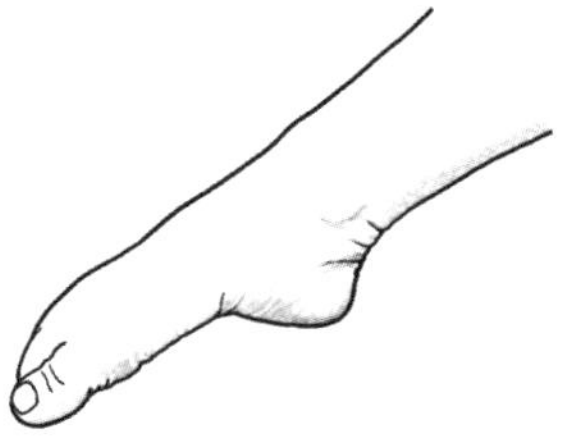

Pointed

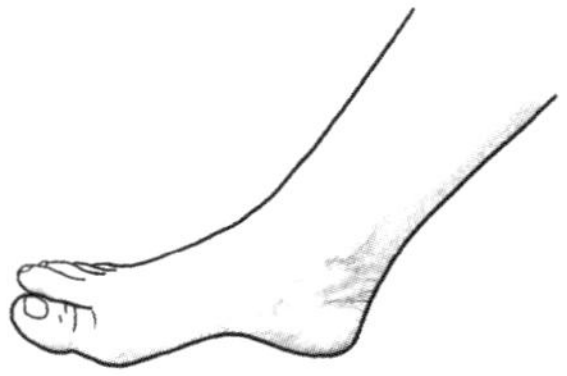

Balance of flexed and pointed

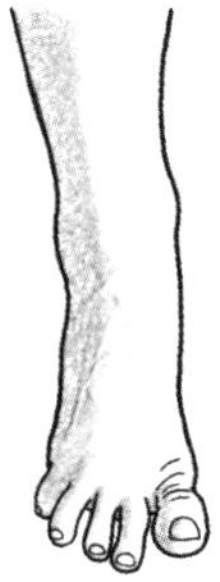

Press out through the big toe mound

Summary: The combined actions of spreading the toes, reaching through the heel, and then pressing out through the ball of the foot create balanced action in the lower leg.

Hands — When Not the Foundation

An active hand helps prāṇic flow, which means hands are important in every pose. To understand the balance of Muscular Engagement and Energetic Extension in the hands, try this:

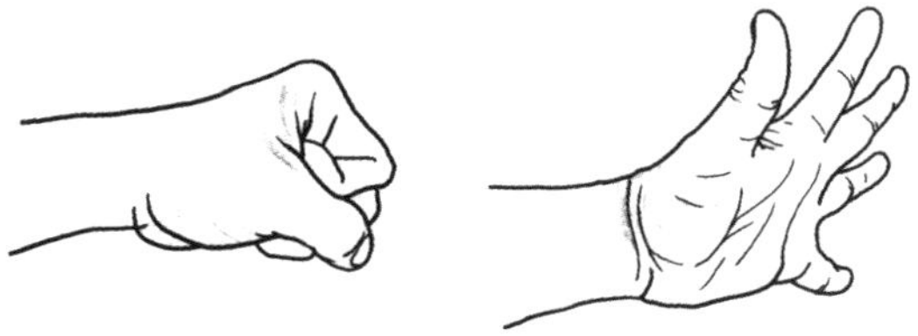

1. Clench your hand into a tight fist. Feel that.
2. Next, open your fingers as long and wide as possible. While the second action has muscularity to it, it is mostly about extension and spaciousness.
3. Now combine the two. First make the fist, then keeping a little of that muscularity to the hand, begin to open the hand and extend the fingers fully. Maintain a balance of muscularity and expansiveness in your hand and extend your arm straight out to the side as in Vīrabhadrāsana II (Warrior II).
4. Let the hand soften (or go limp) and feel the difference in the quality of the whole arm. You may even feel a shift in the energy in the shoulder, chest, neck and face.
5. You can also try these same actions in reverse order: extend and expand your fingers, then activate your palm as if trying to draw your fingers back into a fist without actually curling the fingers in. If it helps, imagine you have your hand spread on top of a basketball that you are trying to press down into a tub of water.

more about feet and hands

closed versus open hands

Closed Versus Open Hands

Some styles of yoga advocate bringing the fingers and toes tightly together when the limbs are extended and not directly part of the foundation. This is not wrong or bad, but there is a qualitative difference when fingers are extended and drawn tightly together or when fingers are extended and spread wide (also true for the feet). According to recent research[4] and in my own experience, spreading the fingers allows for Muscular Engagement and Energetic Expansion and correspondingly opens the energy of the throat and chest.

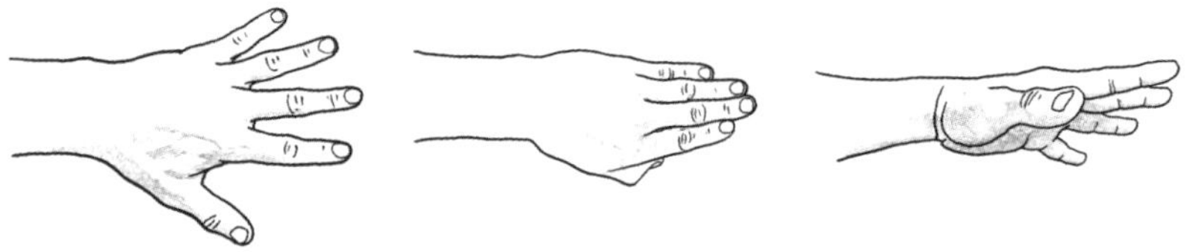

Try this experiment:

1. Extend your arm straight out in front of you at shoulder height or to the side at shoulder height. Make a tight fist. Feel that. Then let your hand go soft. How does that feel different?
2. Now, with the arm in the same extended position, lengthen your fingers and draw them together and tuck your thumb in. Feel that.
3. Then spread your fingers as if palming a basketball or as if your hand were placed for Adho-Mukha Śvanāsana (Downward Facing Dog pose). Feel that. Does it feel different? How and where? Do you notice any subtle difference in the chest or throat?

***Summary**: The hands and feet must have both Muscular Engagement and Energetic Extension occurring at the same time. This is true whether they are part of the foundation or not. The balance of these two energies helps draw your limbs into the core of your body and create radiant extension back out from the core.*

Hands in Standing Poses

When the hands are part of the foundation along with the feet, there are three ways the hands can be placed. Each has a particular purpose and effect.

Hand Flat on the Floor

This position is when the entire hand is on the floor with all four corners grounded, as in Adho-Mukha Śvanāsana (Downward Facing Dog pose). It uses the most surface area of the hand and is very steady and solid.

Ridge Tops

This hand position has all four fingers on the floor with most of the weight being put on the base of the knuckles and the thumb pad. The palm is actively contracted and does not contact the floor. Ridge Tops is often used in poses like Prakramaṇāsana (Lunge pose) or Utthita Trikoṇāsana (Extended Triangle pose). It is very stable and gives more length to the arm. This added length can bring a greater sense of ease and overall extension to a pose.

Finger Tips or Finger Pads

This position adds even more length and sense of extension to the arm in standing poses where the hand meets the floor such as Ardha-Candrāsana (Half Moon pose). The additional length benefits your pose in the same way as Ridge Tops and affords an even greater feeling of Energetic Extension not only in the arm and hand but throughout the pose.

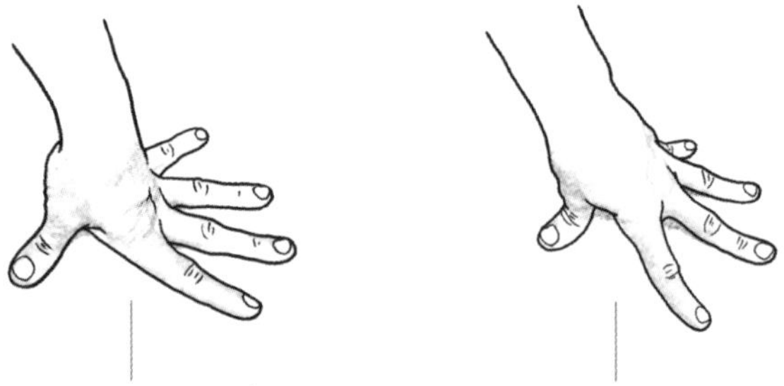

more about feet and hands

binding the hands

What difference does it make?
These three hand positions can make your poses feel significantly different. For example, in Prakramaṇāsana (Lunge pose), if both hands are flat on the floor, the weight of your torso tends to rest more heavily on your front thigh, putting pressure on the diaphragm, inhibiting the breath, and compressing your groin and hip joint of the bent leg. Coming up on your Ridge Tops or Finger Tips can take some of the weight of the chest and belly off the front thigh making breathing easier. This also creates more space at the crease of your hip allowing for more extension in your upper body. Standing poses such as Utthita Pārśvakoṇāsana (Extended Side Angle pose) and Utthita Trikoṇāsana (Extended Triangle pose) benefit in the same way.

There is no right or wrong with these hand variations. Experiment with other poses and notice any differences. They each have different subtle effects on your pose.

Binding the Hands

In several poses, the hands can bind each other or clasp a foot. While this doesn't directly fall under alignment, a bind or a clasp can also vary and influence your experience in a pose.

For example, many seated twists can incorporate a clasping or binding of the hands. In a seated forward fold such as Jānu-Śīrṣāsana (Head to Knee pose) for example, there are several ways you can either clasp the foot or bind the hands around the foot. Each has a different feel and has some influence on the alignment of the pose. The reason I even raise this issue is that you may see or be taught bound hands in a variety of poses. In seated twists binding the hands can create a sense of firmness and stability in the posture. A bind also tends to add pressure on the shoulder joints as well as the torso, potentially inhibiting your breath. In seated forward folds, a bind may encourage us to compromise our alignment or push too hard to achieve it. Binds are a fairly advanced expression of a pose. If you are working towards binds in poses, shoulder alignment is very important. I also suggest using a yoga strap as you first attempt binds, rather than struggle or push to achieve a difficult position. Using a strap will allow you to explore while minimizing any risk of injury.

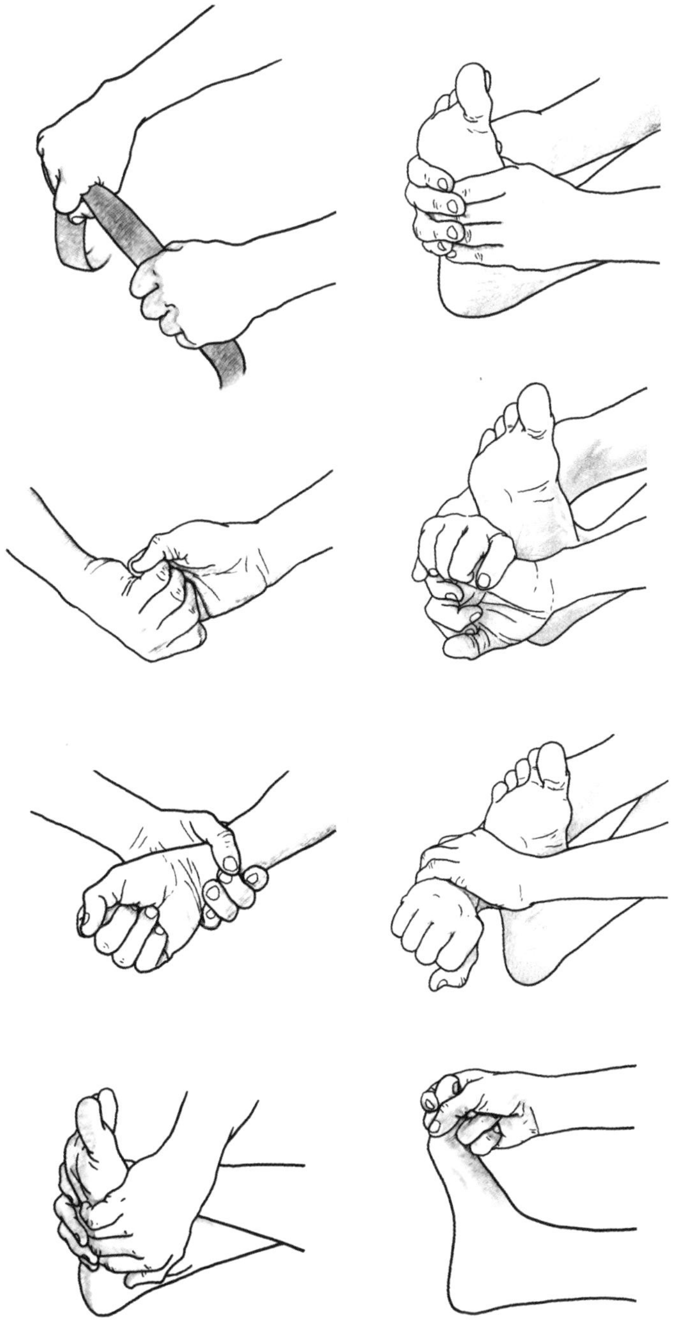

stretching
active versus passive

Active Versus Passive Stretching

Many people assume that relaxing the muscles while stretching allows them to lengthen more. But passively stretching muscles can strain the ligaments and the attachment or insertion of the muscle (where the muscles are connected to the bone). This can lead to injury. Engaging the muscles first and maintaining engagement for the duration of the stretch helps distribute the load more evenly throughout the muscle. For example, with a seated forward bend such as Paścimottānāsana (Seated Forward Fold), it is important to first initiate all of the principles of the legs and pelvis particularly Muscular Engagement, hugging to the midline and activating Energetic Extension before proceeding with a stretch. Actively engaging in this way also ensures the legs stay aligned and in the same position throughout the duration of the stretch.

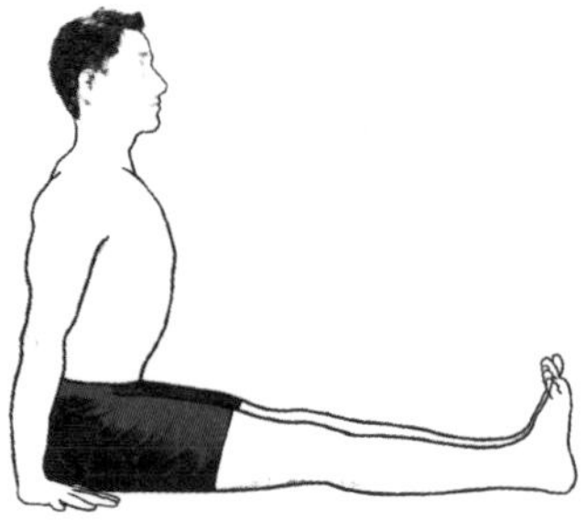

Firm the legs with Muscular Engagement

Maintain Muscular Engagement, extend torso

Flexibility and Range of Movement

Along with our habitual movement patterns, our genetics and body type play a big part in how flexible we are, especially when we first begin practicing yoga āsana. Over time, as our mind and body forge a deeper connection through the practice, our flexibility can increase rather dramatically.

We've probably all been in a class of beginners with the "stiff person" on one side and the "super bendy" person on the other. Experience and physiology both contribute to their abilities. Factors such as muscle mass, muscle density, intrinsic length of muscle tissue, quality of connective tissue, thickness of disc tissue in the spine—just to mention a few—are part of our inherent physiology, the body we were born with. Even intrinsic *kinesthetic*[5] awareness and *proprioception*[6] may have a genetic component. These genetic factors have an effect on initial range of motion, strength, stability and balance. With consistent practice we can increase strength, flexibility, balance and coordination. This period of change will be longer for some and shorter for others. Remember: it isn't about how deep or extreme you get in a pose or how you compare to another—yoga is your own personal journey.

alignment and the breath

the supportive breath

The breath is one of your greatest tools in āsana practice. The breath connects the mind to our movement and supports the flow of energy throughout the body. The proper use of breath generates strength and supports openness and freedom in yoga poses. It harmonizes the balance of effort and ease within the poses and continuously connects us to a bigger energy.

During yoga āsana, it is important to breathe through your nose rather than your mouth. Breathing through your nose allows for a smoother, more even breath, calming and grounding the nervous system. Breathing from your mouth, on the other hand, fires up the nervous system.

Both the *parasympathetic* nervous system and the *sympathetic* nervous system are affected by the breath. When stimulated, the parasympathetic nervous system tends to lower blood pressure and heart rate while bringing relaxation to the body and mind. Stimulating the sympathetic nervous system does the exact opposite, sending more glucose (fuel) to the muscles, elevating the heart rate and blood pressure, and inhibiting digestion. In short, it prepares the body for the "fight or flight" response.

Sympathetic nervous system responses are useful things if you have to run from an angry mastodon you've just poked with a spear. But in yoga, we want to activate the parasympathetic nervous system to reduce stress in the mind and body and cultivate balance. In essence we are looking to cultivate *Sattva*, a classical term meaning evenness, luminosity, joy, purity or deep knowledge.

Inhale

With regard to the alignment principles, we initiate Muscular Engagement with the inhale of breath. Try this:

1. In a standing pose, consciously grip the floor with your feet. Hug the muscles of the legs to the bone, then draw the whole leg upward toward the core of the pelvis.
2. On an inhale, feel the expansion and lift of the rib cage and spine.

Exhale

On our exhale, we initiate Energetic Extension, extending from the core lines of the torso out through the limbs. In Vīrabhadrāsana II (Warrior II), for example, once we have brought Muscular Engagement to our arms, we can then use the exhale to expand, and thus initiate twists and side bends.

Quality of Breath

Unconscious breathing habits may affect the quality of our āsana practice. *Upper chest breathing* is a relatively shallow breath that does not make full use of the lungs. Upper chest breathing may also be associated with unnecessary tension held in the jaw, throat, and chest. Another habit is *belly breathing*, in which we do not fully use our lungs. If we become conscious of our whole torso when breathing, we can correct these habits and breath more fully.

For a full, even breath:

1. Relax and bring a feeling of soft spaciousness to your mouth, throat, and upper chest.
2. Start your inhale down deep in the belly and let it rise to fullness at the top of your chest.
3. On the exhale, let your breath empty smoothly out from the top of your chest down to your lower abdomen.
4. Be aware of any tendency to hold your breath, which can happen when we are too focused on the actions of a pose. Holding your breath is also a sign that you may be straining or over exerting in a pose. It not only robs your body of oxygen, but also can create unnecessary tension and agitate your mind.

We can't really talk about breath and the actions in āsana without talking about *prāṇa*, our internal life force. The breath and prāṇa are inextricably linked. More on prāṇa and its role in our yoga practice will be discussed in the following section.

prana and alignment

fundamentals of pranic movement

Can I practice āsana without knowing about prāṇa? Is understanding how this energy moves in the body really important? These are valid questions and the answer is yes. You can do all the mechanical actions in āsana without having any knowledge of prāṇa. These actions are helping you optimize the flow of prāṇa whether you are aware of it or not. What you will begin to discover is that when you do have some understanding of how prāṇa moves, you can use the alignment principles described in this book to an even greater effect, enhancing the power, balance and openness within your poses. Each pose will sparkle and vibrate with added vigor and poise that would otherwise feel unavailable.

Fundamentals of Pranic Movement

Now that we have covered the fundamental alignment principles, I think it's important to introduce and define prāṇa. We'll look at how it naturally moves in the body and how this energy relates to the various alignment principles. We'll be using some classical terms to describe how prāṇa has been observed to naturally move and function in the body. At first these terms and concepts may seem abstract, mystical, and a little esoteric. But ultimately they will help you see how your internal energy flows and how you can consciously direct it with your mind. You may have already heard some of these terms in a yoga class or come across them in reading. I will define them clearly here and explain how they link in a practical way to the alignment principles.

Prana Vayus - The Winds of Life

Though there is only one life-force, Mahāprāṇa, or Great Prāṇa, it moves and functions in distinct ways in the body. These distinct functions or movements are called *vāyus*. *Vāyu* is a Sanskrit word meaning "wind." The root of the word *va* means "that which flows," so a vāyu is a vehicle for activities and experiences within the body, or a force that moves throughout the system in specific ways. There are five major vāyus that are of particular significance and value to your yoga practice. They are: *Prāṇa vāyu, Apāṇa vāyu, Samāna vāyu, Udāna vāyu,* and *Vyāna vāyu*. Together they are called the *Pañca Vāyus*, or "Five Winds."

Conceptually breaking down Mahāprāṇa into five distinct vāyus helps describe how this one, all-pervasive prāṇic energy moves in diverse regions of the body and functions in the body's various processes. Yet together the Pañca Vāyus operate as a coordinated whole and are still ultimately Mahāprāṇa, just in different forms serving certain purposes.

Prāṇa vāyu and Apāṇa vāyu
Prāṇa vāyu is the ascending energy current in the front of the body creating an expansive lift. Apāṇa vāyu is the descending, grounding energy current of the lower body.

Samāna vāyu (moving in)
This is a balancing and harmonizing energy current for the other vāyus. Prāṇa gathers at this center, creating more integration and cohesion for the entire body.

Samāna vāyu (moving out)
The other vāyus connect and move out from this center as a focal or anchor point known as the Kanda.

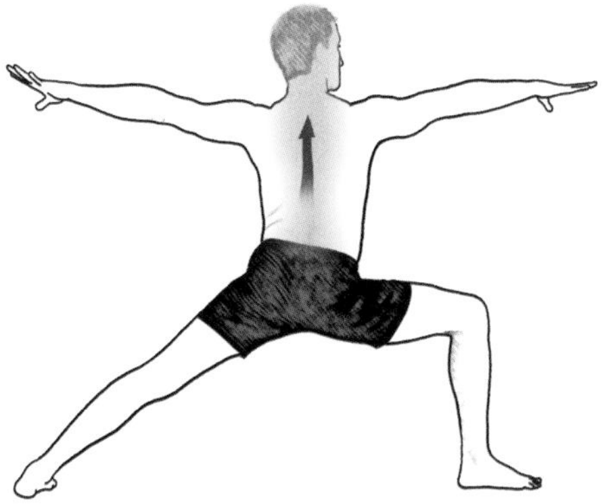

Udāna vāyu
Moving up the back of the body, this energy is responsible for maintaining an upright posture.

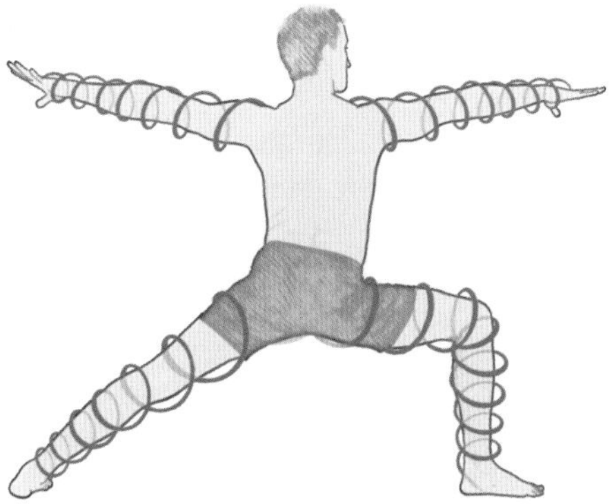

Vyāna vāyu
Pervades the whole body. It moves in the limbs in a spiraling action creating strength and supporting expansion.

prana and alignment
fundamentals of pranic movement

How Prana Moves in the Body

The Five Prāṇa Vāyus move in the body like this:

1. The Downward Current
The downward moving energy current in the body is called Apāṇa vāyu. It emanates from the core of the pelvis and extends down through the legs to the feet. It is a powerful grounding and stabilizing force that connects to Energetic Extension in our lower half. Apāṇa directly correlates to Energetic Extension in the legs and feet.

2. The Upward Currents
There are two upward moving energy currents, Prāṇa vāyu and Udāna vāyu. Prāṇa vāyu flows up the front of the torso, lifting and expanding the front body. Udāna vāyu rises up the back of the torso, lengthening the spine up to the crown of the head. It secondarily connects to the arms when they extend out from the torso. Together Apāṇa and Prāṇa vāyus are responsible for Energetic Extension in the torso, neck and upper limbs.

3. The Equalizing Current
The fourth energy current is Samāna vāyu. Samāna vāyu is centered around the navel area and is the juncture where the upward and downward moving currents connect and move out from. Samāna correlates with the principles of the pelvis.

4. The Integrating Current
A fifth energy current, Vyāna vāyu, is responsible for general muscle function. It has a connection to the principle of Muscular Engagement. This current is a cohesive, integrating energy that pervades and radiates throughout the whole body and supports expansion.

***Summary**: Prāṇa pervades the entire body, yet there are distinct ways in which it flows and affects various areas. The internal energetic flow moves down from the pelvis to the feet and up from the pelvis to the top of the head. This prāṇic flow supports the physical efforts of the body.*

Try this: Sit in Daṇḍāsana (Staff pose). Muscularly engage the legs. From the foundation, extend the torso upward. Try and maintain the lift and let the legs go soft. What happens in the upper body? Did you notice diminished energy and extension? Now, engage and lift again. This time let the upper body soften and sink. What happens to the energy in the legs? When we generate the downward current, it helps support the upward current and visa versa.

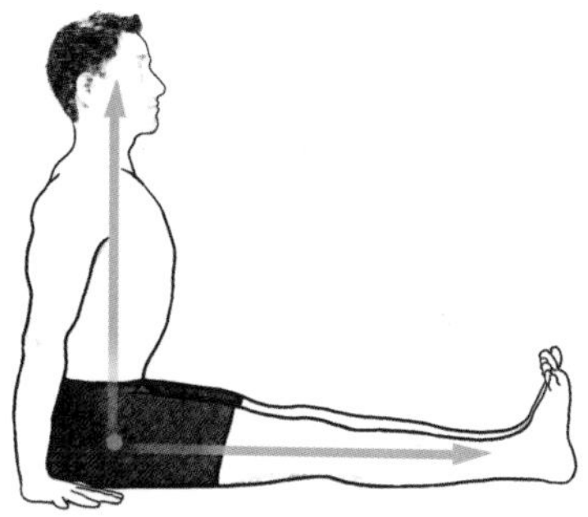

prana and alignment
mula bandha and uddiyana bandha

Mula Bandha and Uddiyana Bandha
The Energy Keystones

The two Sanskrit terms, *Mūla Bandha* and *Uḍḍīyāna Bandha*, together describe the method of connecting the downward energy current with the upward currents, Apāṇa vāyu with Prāṇa and Udāna vāyus. Combined, they are the means to harness and direct the power of the Pañca Vāyus (Five Winds). Establishing the bandhas correlates directly to the alignment actions of the legs and pelvis. So from this perspective, the bandhas are a short hand for the various actions and principles of the lower body. These actions are also the conscious recruitment of Samāna vāyu and its role in connecting Apāṇa vāyu with Prāṇa and Udāna vāyus.

Mūla Bandha translates from Sanskrit as "Root Loch." It is formed at the floor of the pelvis from the actions of the upper thighs first moving back and apart, then the tailbone lengthening down. Uḍḍīyāna Bandha, or "Flying-up Loch" is the internal drawing in and up of the very lower abdomen from the actions made lower down by the legs and tailbone.

Here is how to create Mūla Bandha (Root Loch) and Uḍḍīyāna Bandha (Flying-up Loch) using the techniques for the legs described earlier.

1. Firm the muscles in your legs then press into the vertical midline with the feet and lower legs.
2. Next rotate your upper inner thighs back and apart, widening the sit bones and floor of your pelvis.
3. Draw your tailbone down and your pubic bone up (pelvic floor domes subtly upward).
4. Draw your lower abdomen in and up and draw your lower ribs back.

When you engage these four actions in this order, you help lift and expand the upper part of your back and create a powerful, internal connection between the lower and upper parts of your body.

***Note**: I translate bandha as "loch" rather than the usual lock. Lock describes a holding, blocking or closing. By contrast, loch connotes a channeling of flow or redirecting of movement. This is a more accurate description of what the various bandhas are in fact doing.*

Standing Poses

Standing poses offer one of the best ways to practice and embody the full range of alignment principles. Physically, standing poses cultivate the greatest degree of strength, flexibility, balance, and poise. Psychologically, they engender determination, courage, confidence, and mental alertness.

Width of Stance

How far apart you place your feet on any given standing pose relates to the proportions of your body. Here's one rule of thumb for finding the optimal balance between stability and freedom in any standing pose:

1. Stand sideways on your mat with your arms extended out at shoulder height.
2. Widen your legs so that your ankles are directly under your wrists, with your feet in parallel position.

This is the basic distance apart for your feet in any standing pose. If this standing width is difficult at first, while you are building strength in your legs, you can bring your feet closer together for more stability. With time and practice, widen your stance.

Another good rule of thumb is to always adjust the width of your stance with your rear leg. In Vīrabhadrāsana I (Warrior I) for example, your front leg is more stable, so adjust your stance by moving your back leg closer in or farther away.

Balance of Rotation

In most standing poses each leg is in a different position, one leg front and one leg behind. Also, in the majority of standing poses, one leg is bent while the other is straight. This basic geometry naturally influences the position of your pelvis. The position of your front leg will cause your pelvis to angle differently than the position of your back leg. As a general guideline, *your rear leg requires more of an inward rotation at the upper inner thigh, while your front thigh has a predominantly outer rotation emphasis*. This encourages your hips to even out or "square," whether square to the front in a pose such as Vīrabhadrāsana I (Warrior I), or square to the side in a pose such as Vīrabhadrāsana II (Warrior II). It is the same for all revolved standing poses. (Refer to basics of leg alignment on page 19.)

***Note**: Lateral poses may get taught with the rear foot turned inward toward 45 degrees. In my experience, however, this can create too much inward rotation of the rear leg, causing the front or crest of the pelvis on the rear leg side to turn too far forward. Such a stance can compromise the angle of the pelvis and cause the torso above to face more forward than sideways. This tends to cause the front leg to also have more inner rotation (when we are looking to have predominantly outer rotation in the front leg). It deepens the groin at the front hip joint causing compression and making it more difficult to open or broaden the front thigh.*

With back foot at 45 degree angle back leg overly rotates inward. Groin closes at hip joint. ⃠

Back foot parallel to back edge of mat gives more balanced rotation. Front groin more open.

specifics of alignment in each category of pose

floor poses

In this exercise we'll reiterate the sequence for balanced action in the legs and pelvis using a modified Uttitha Pārśvakoṇāsana (Extend Side Angle pose). This will help you to translate the basic sequence of actions for standing poses.

1. Back foot parallel to the back edge of the mat.
2. Front foot facing straight forward in line with the center of the shin.
3. With Muscular Engagement, isometrically draw your legs toward each other (vertical midline).
4. Rotate your upper, inner thighs back and apart.
5. Sit bones lift and broaden. Top of sacrum tilts forward. Floor of pelvis broadens.
6. Keep that and lengthen tailbone down.
7. Pubic bone lifts. Floor of pelvis draws up. Lower abdomen firms and draws in and up.
8. Turn the upper torso and extend the top arm

***Summary**: Balanced action in your legs means equal amounts of Muscular Engagement with Energetic Extension. In any standing pose, the thigh of your rear leg should work to inwardly rotate, while the thigh of your front leg should work to rotate outwardly to bring balance and clear orientation to the pelvis and upper body.*

Floor Poses

Many floor poses require both the feet and hands as their foundation, such as Caturaṅga Daṇḍāsana (Four Points Staff pose) or Adho-Mukha Śvanāsana (Downward Facing Dog). In other floor poses, such as seated forward folds and supine postures, the hands and feet play less of a direct role as part of the foundation. Yet in any floor pose, you work the legs in the same way that you would in Tāḍāsana (Mountain pose), creating a balance of Muscular Engagement and Energetic Extension. The upper inner thighs are rotated back and apart and the tailbone is lengthened. The actions of the legs and pelvis in this way will always generate more stability in the lower limbs thus connecting to the upper body for greater stability as well as extension and freedom of movement of the spine. The actions of the shoulders are also the same as they are in Tāḍāsana: the side of the body lengthens, the shoulders move up away from the hips, and then toward the back plane.

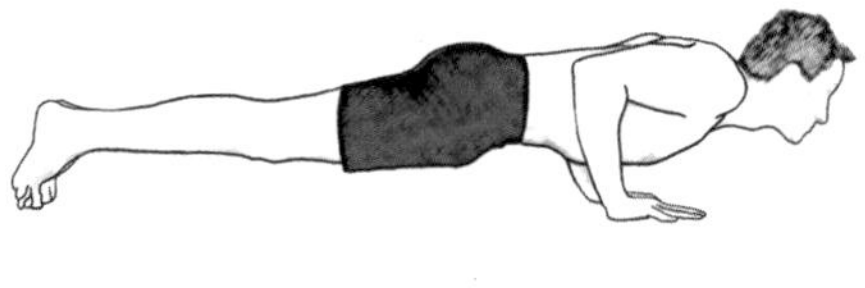

Caturaṅga Daṇḍāsana

Adho-Mukha Śvanāsana

Building Adho-Mukha Śvanāsana

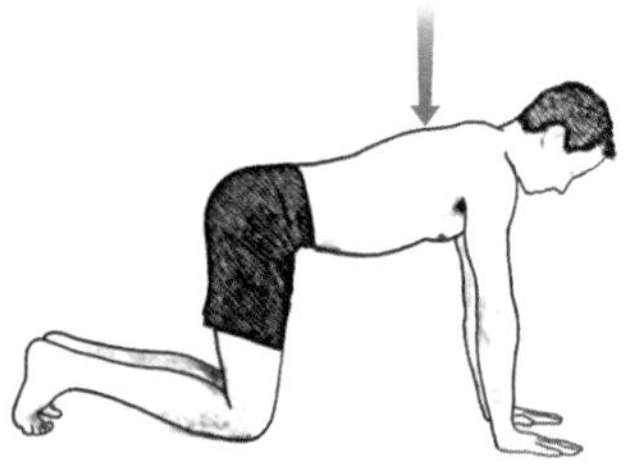

Lengthen torso. Lower chest bringing the shoulder blades on the back.

Keep actions in shoulders, lift knees from floor. Sit bones lift and broaden. Inwardly rotate thighs.

Keep actions of the legs and straighten. Top of thighs back. Base of shins back. Upper arms lift while chest moves down.

Building Caturaṅga Daṇḍāsana

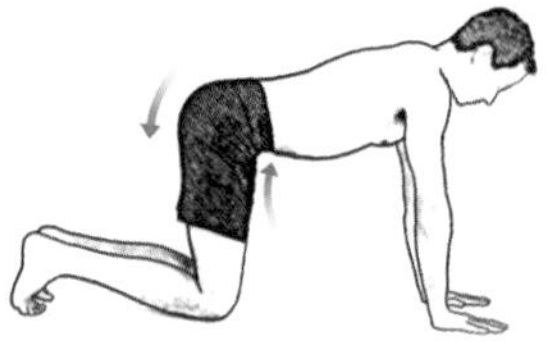

Lengthen torso. Lower chest, bring shoulder blades onto the back. Inwardly rotate thighs, lengthen tailbone down. Tone lower belly.

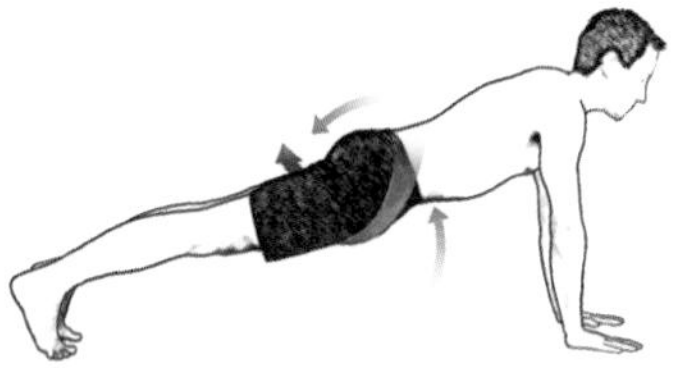

Keep first actions, move to Phalakāsana (Plank), reaffirm tailbone, firm lower abdomen. Legs strong.

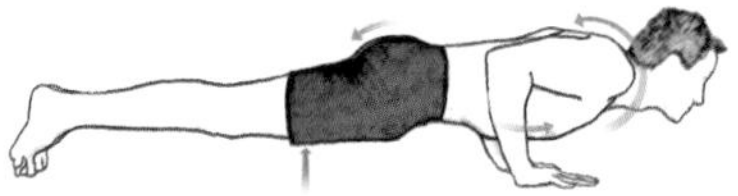

Maintain all actions and lower to Caturaṅga Daṇḍāsana.

specifics of alignment in each category of pose
forward folds

Forward Folds

Your legs and pelvis (sitting bones) form the foundation in forward folds. Work the legs and pelvis as described for Tāḍāsana (Mountain pose). Maintain Muscular Engagement in your straight leg and Energetic Extension in both the straight and bent leg. With your heel grounding and extending, spread your toes and press through the big toe mound. The strength and groundedness in the lower body generates length upward out of the foundation giving your torso more reach out over the legs. When clasping the shins, ankles, or feet, use your arms to simply help guide you forward and extend your waist and upper body. Avoid grabbing your feet and pulling yourself forward and down. This will contract and shorten the muscles in your torso, creating a sense of compression and strain. It also tends to pull the shoulder blades off the back. Simply use your arms to encourage your waist and torso to lengthen forward while maintaining the alignment for the shoulders. The back of your pelvis will tilt forward, as your spine curves with length, evenly and gradually. On an inhale lift and extend your torso. With the exhale, bow out over your leg. Avoid over-tucking your chin and instead lengthen the top of your head as an extension of your spine.

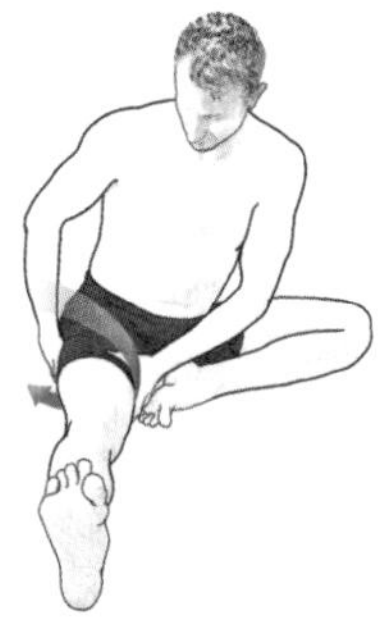

Inwardly rotate the upper inner thigh and widen the buttock, then engage the leg. Balanced action in the feet.

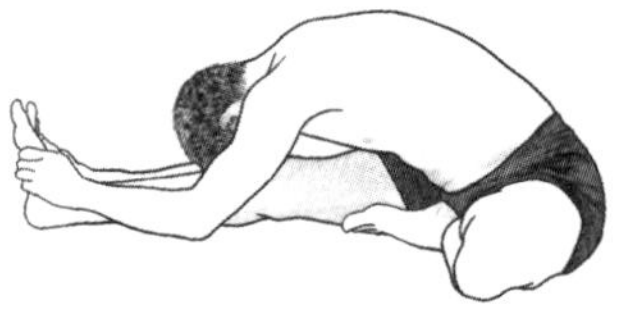

Pulling yourself down into a forward fold shortens the torso and brings the shoulder blades off the back. ⦸

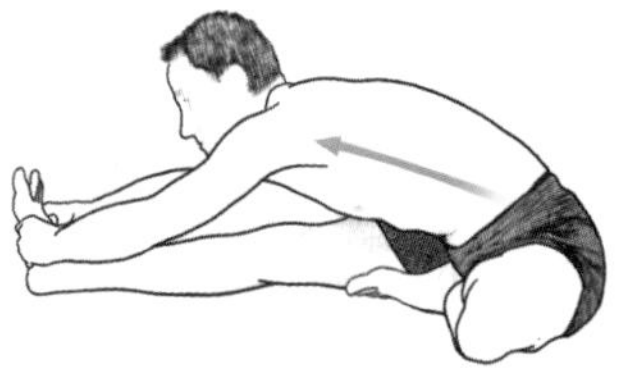

Lift the elbows, bring the shoulder blades onto the back and extend forward from the foundation.

Twists

Twists benefit the muscles and connective tissue around the spine and rib cage and revitalize and cleanse the internal organs. They are initiated deep in the core of your pelvis using the bandhas.

In a seated twist:

1. Create a solid stable foundation with even weight in your sit bones (ischial tuberosities).
2. Use the rising energy of your inhale to generate length upward from the foundation. The longer you can make your spine, creating space between the vertebrae, the more ease and depth you will have in twists.
3. Initiate length in your spine on an inhale then initiate the twist on an exhale, without losing that length. Inhale lift, exhale twist.
4. Use your arms to help steer the twist further into your chest and shoulders, letting your head simply follow. Avoid leading the twist from your head or cranking your head around too far.

The more length you create in the spine, the deeper and more easeful your twist. Inhale lift, exhale twist. Prāṇa and Udāna vāyus are the forces at play to support the torso.

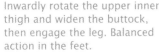

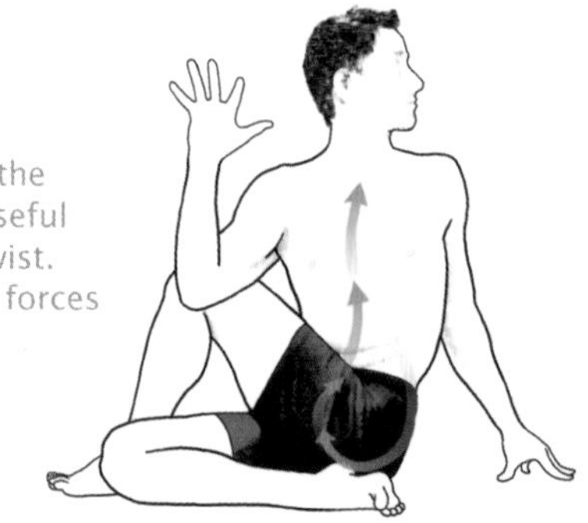

Hip Openers

The bones and muscles of your hips and legs are among the largest and strongest in your body. Consequently, they may also be among the tightest. Your hips are a ball and socket joint, and so the legs potentially have a very wide range of motion. To access and develop that range with proper alignment is key.

specifics of alignment in each category of pose

arm balances

When doing hip opening poses, try using your hands to help establish proper alignment in your legs and pelvis.

Using Baddha Koṇāsana (Bound Angle pose) as an example, here's how to do the manual adjustment.

1. Place one hand on the flesh of the upper inner thigh, and the other under the buttock on the same side.
2. Turn the flesh of the upper inner thigh downward with your hands and widen back away from the midline.
3. Now widen the under side of the buttock back and away from the midline. This action helps the femur bones descend, sets the femur bone more deeply in the socket, and creates space at the hip flexor. It makes the floor of the pelvis broader and more spacious.
4. Adding a subtle downward "lengthening" of the tailbone and a drawing in and up of the lower abdomen helps you engage Mūla Bandha and Uḍḍīyāna Bandha, which releases tension in the lower back and makes it easier to sit up with more length (see illustration).
5. Maintain length in your waist and the forward tilt of your sacrum as your torso bows forward, as in any forward bend.

Turning the thighs helps descend the femurs and soften the groins.

Protecting the Knees in Hip Openers

The knee joint is a smaller joint than the hip and has less range of motion. Because of the strength and potential tightness of the hips, knee joints can be vulnerable to strain. To avoid knee strain, spread your toes and keep them spread during hip openers. This action fires the muscles in your lower leg and helps stabilize your knee and ankle. You can go deep in hip openers as long as you maintain the stability of the knees and keep them free of discomfort. Always start with basic hip openers and move toward deeper more complex ones.

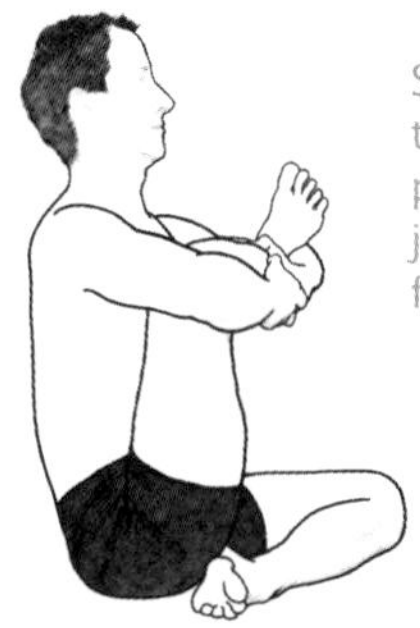

Spreading the toes helps protect the knee joint. Keep ankle firm not curved.

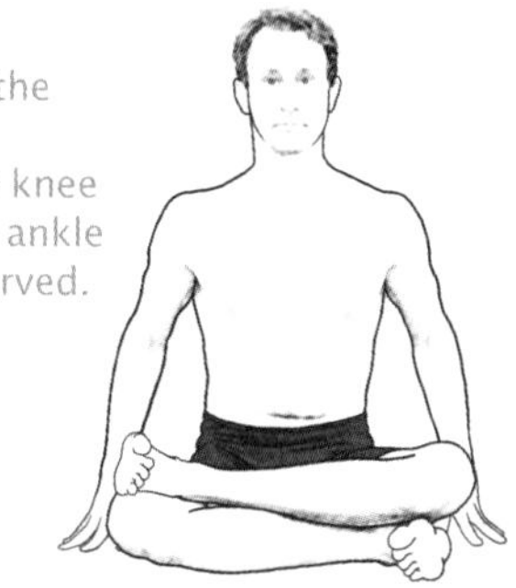

Arm Balances

Arm balances are relatively complex poses that require both Muscular Engagement and Energetic Extension with a strong focus on drawing into the midline. Because of the strength and flexibility they require, Arm balances can engender profound self-confidence. Poses such as Adho-Mukha Śvanāsana (Downward Facing Dog), Caturaṅga Daṇḍāsana (Four Points Staff pose), and Urdhva Mukha Śvanāsana (Upward Facing Dog) can help us develop the necessary strength for arm balances.

Here are some important things to remember when doing arm balances:

1. Spread your toes and strongly work the feet. This will bring Muscular Engagement to your pose.
2. Powerful work with the tailbone and lower abdominal engagement along with firmly drawing into the midline is critical for success in arm balances (see section on Bandhas on page 34).
3. Breathe. Breathing in arm balances is often challenging because we are concentrating so hard and focusing on power. But holding your breath robs your muscles of much-needed oxygen and will quickly weaken your body.

Develop your awareness in arm balances. Build gradually and remember that every attempt plants a seed that will grow if you cultivate it.

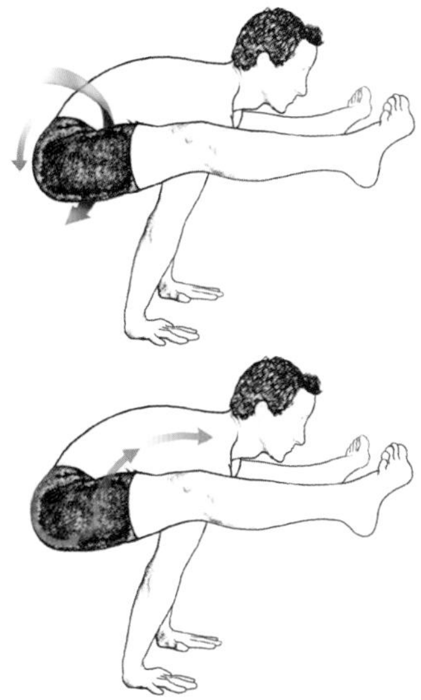

Maintain firm Mūla bandha and Uḍḍīyāna throughout. Breathe!

specifics of alignment in each category of pose

backbends

Backbends

Backbends open the whole front of the body, particularly the chest, thighs, and groins. Backbends develop tremendous flexibility in the spine and great strength in the upper back, shoulders, and legs. The lungs and breathing muscles of the ribcage are opened improving overall breathing capacity. The energy channels along the spine are opened and the flow of Prāṇa in the body, particularly in the area of the heart is significantly enhanced. Emotional blocks are most often released through backbends, opening the way for the positive qualities of courage, enthusiasm, adventurousness, joy, and trust in yourself to expand.

In all backbends, lengthening the spine from the start is critical. As with twists, lengthening the spine creates more space between the individual vertebrae allowing more range of motion. We can do this with our breath and from the solid grounding of the foundation. Actions for proper shoulder alignment are also very important in backbends, as are the principles of alignment for the legs and pelvis.

Below are the alignment actions for two basic backbends, Setu-Bandha Sarvāṅgāsana (Bridge Building pose) and Ūrdhva Dhanurāsana (Upward Bow pose).

Setu-Bandha Sarvāṅgāsana (Bridge Building Pose)
This backbend has a very stable foundation and is a good place to learn to coordinate the various alignment techniques used in all backbends.

1. Lie on your back with your knees bent. Place your feet flat on the floor, parallel to one another, a few inches away from your buttocks. Make the outer edges of your feet even with your outer hips.
2. While on your back, inhale and "walk" your shoulders up away from your hips, creating length in the torso. Maintain that length and bring the top of your shoulders toward the back plane of the body and down firmly to the floor. The tips of your shoulder blades move up and in toward the bottom of your heart. Expand your chest with fullness.
3. Inwardly rotate your upper, inner thighs and lengthen your tailbone.
4. Keeping these actions, raise your hips on an inhale. Draw your heels gently back (toward the head) to engage your hamstrings. Avoid pushing your hips up with strong contraction in the buttocks. This diminishes your ability to evenly lengthen your spine and decreases flexibility in your upper back. It also impinges prāṇic flow in the back in general.
5. Lift your chest from behind your heart, keeping your chin neutral (neither tucked in or thrown back).
6. Straighten your arms under you and clasp your hands together. Firmly ground your upper arms and wrists into the floor. Lift through the sides of the upper rib cage while moving your upper arms and shoulders down.
7. With this solid grounding of the shoulders, reaffirm the inner rotation of the legs balanced with the lengthening of the tailbone toward the knees. Again, these actions of the inner thighs and tailbone are subtle and not initiated with strong contraction of the buttocks.
8. To come out of the pose, release the pelvis down first, followed by the chest and shoulders.

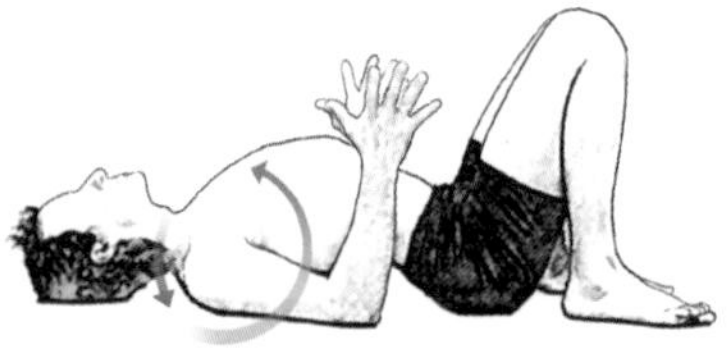
Lengthen torso, shoulders toward floor, full chest.

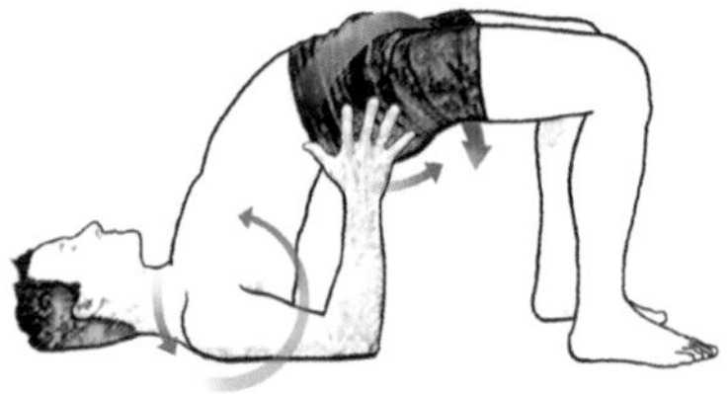
Keep chest full, raise the pelvis. Don't over engage buttocks.

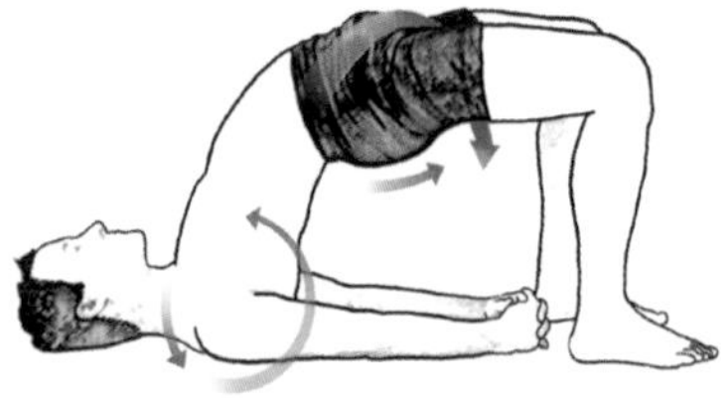
Ground shoulders, lift chest from behind the heart. Keep throat free.

Lower hips back down.

Ūrdhva Dhanurāsana (Upward Facing Bow Pose)
Proper alignment in Ūrdhva Dhanurāsana is built on the work done in Setu-Bandha Sarvāṅgāsana (Bridge Building pose).

1. While on your back, bend your elbows and place your hands on the floor on either side of the head, your wrists in line with the ears, fingers pointing toward the shoulders.
2. Follow the steps for setting up Setu-Bandha Sarvāṅgāsana, including raising your hips.
3. With your hips raised, move to the top of your head on an inhale. Widen the hands to the edges of the mat. Reaffirm the principles of the shoulders and draw back from your elbows to your shoulders, keeping your shoulder blades well on your back.
4. Fill your torso with the breath and on an exhale press into the hands, straighten your arms, and lift your torso.
5. Once up, continue to extend your fingers and press them down into your mat. Keep encouraging the outer edges of your shoulder blades back and the head of your upper arm back. Extend your arms straight, lengthening your inner arm down toward the base of your thumb. This helps your elbows from bowing away from the midline.
6. Notice if your buttocks are over working. Soften your groins and lengthen your tailbone, drawing your pubic bone toward the chest.
7. To come down, bend your elbows, tuck your chin to your chest, and lower to your shoulders. Release your hips to the floor.

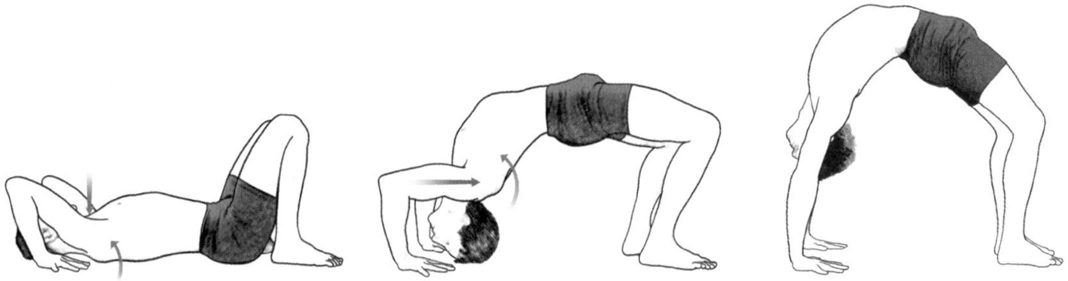

Inversions

Classically, inversions were seen primarily as a method to encourage prāṇic flow up the Suṣumṇā Nāḍi, the central spiritual channel of the body (more details in *The Yoga Practice Guide, Volume 2*). Inversions also have physiological benefits such as enhanced lymphatic drainage, general glandular revitalization, and enhanced blood flow to the brain. They also develop balance in the body and equipoise of the mind with a general soothing effect on both.

We'll use two poses, Sālamba Śīrṣāsana I (Headstand) and Sālamba Sarvāṅgāsana (Shoulderstand), to guide you through alignment principles.

Sālamba Śīrṣāsana I (Headstand)
Seeing Sālamba Śīrṣāsana I as an upside-down Tāḍāsana will go a long way in informing your pose, as the alignment principles are essentially identical. The foundation in Sālamba Śīrṣāsana is made up of the little finger edge of the hands, wrists, forearms and crown of the head. An equilateral triangle shape is made with head, hands, forearms, and elbows.

Position 1

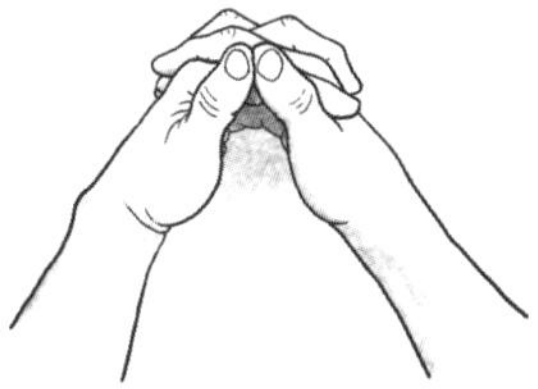
Position 2

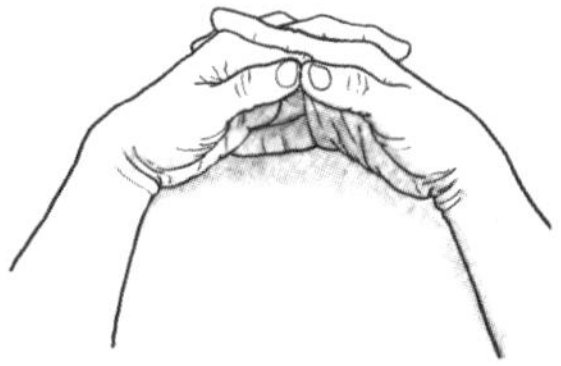
Position 3

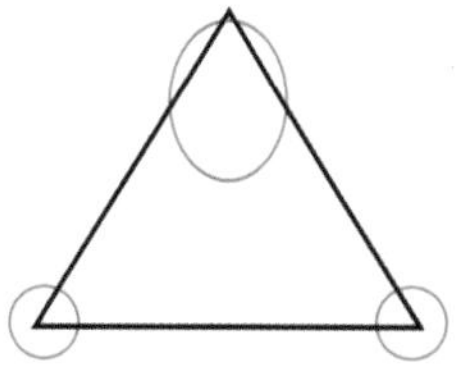
Head and elbows form equilateral triangle.

Three basic hand positions can be used for Sālamba Śīrṣāsana I. Position one, though the most narrow, facilitates the greatest grounding and stability of the hands, wrists, and forearms. Position two allows solid grounding of the hands and wrists while widening the base formed by the forearms. Position three is less heavily grounded in the hands and wrist but allows for more softness and mobility in the shoulders. Positions one and two are appropriate for beginning students, while position three is for more seasoned practitioners. Also, beginners should start practicing Sālamba Śīrṣāsana I at a wall.

1. Set the foundation on your hands and knees with your forearms on the floor, elbows shoulder width apart and the fingers interlaced right up to the webbing. Place your knuckles at the wall. Make sure the edges of your hands and wrists have full contact with the floor and your fingers are not strongly gripped.
2. Extend your head in line with your spine, eyes gazing at your hands.

specifics of alignment in each category of pose

inversions

3. Take a few full breaths to bring an expansive energy into your torso.
4. Soften your chest down allowing your shoulder blades to move more onto your back. Your belly and lower back will tend to collapse here so add a little downward movement of your tailbone to firm your belly and draw the belly up away from the floor, as if filling your kidney area with air.
5. Maintain this and place the top of your head on the floor with the back of your head against the base of your thumbs (illustration).
6. Maintaining the position of your shoulder blades, lift your hips as in Adho-Mukha Śvanāsana (Downward Facing Dog pose).
7. With straight legs, tiptoe your feet toward your hands getting the hips as vertical as possible. Keep your shoulders over your elbows, and don't allow them to roll toward the wall!
8. Connect to the breath, keep your shoulders set, and on an exhale, swing one leg up as straight and extended as possible. Immediately follow with the other leg. Once up, press your legs together firmly to the vertical midline. Maintain Muscular Engagement with Energetic Extension in the legs.
9. Even upside down, align your legs and pelvis as if standing in Tāḍāsana. This will help you engage Mūla Bandha and Uḍḍīyāna Bandha.
10. Once your body is vertical, give your unwavering attention to the vertical midline. Stretch down into the crown of your head. From there, extend everything else up. Try not to overwork your shoulders and neck. They should remain relatively soft. Keep your wrists firmly pressing into the floor yet let your shoulders be loose and light. Think of the arms as the training wheels of a bicycle, providing lateral stability but not supporting all the weight.
11. Come down from headstand in reverse order, one straight leg at a time.
12. Rest in Balāsana (Child's pose).

***Note**: If you have tight hamstrings, it might be more difficult to kick up with straight legs. In this case, once your hips are raised in preparation, swing your first leg up in a bent position bringing that foot to the wall. Follow with your other leg, also bent. Once up, keep both knees bent with the bottoms of your feet touching the wall. Establish your balance, establish your breath, then extend your legs up the wall and press them gently but steadily toward the midline.*

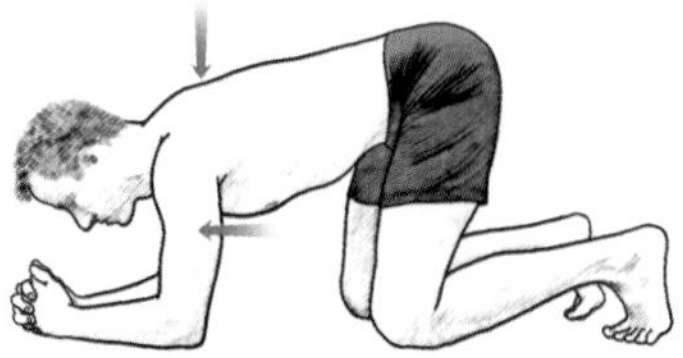

Head of the arm bone forward, sink the chest toward the floor. Shoulder blades on the back.

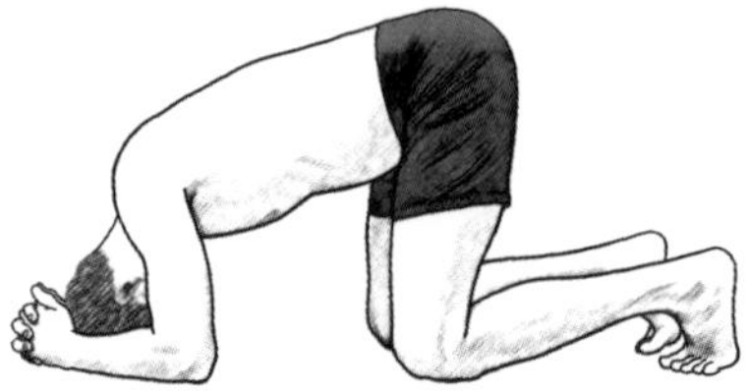

Maintain first actions, place the head.

Lift the hips, reaffirm the shoulders.

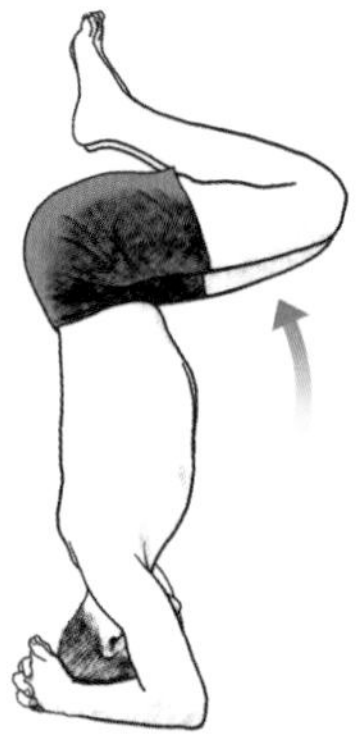

Lightly jump the legs to a tucked position

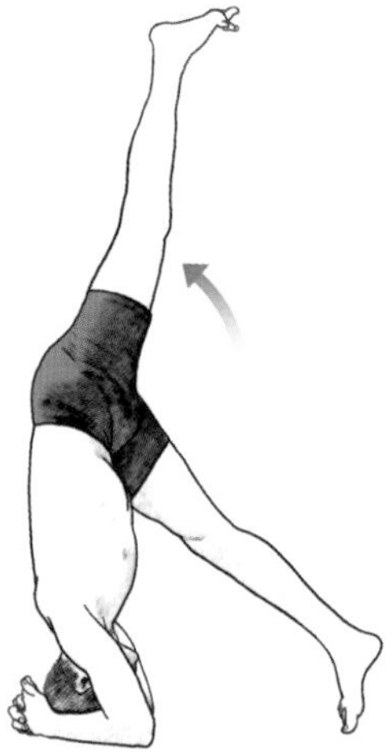

Alternatively, keep legs straight and extend one leg up at a time.

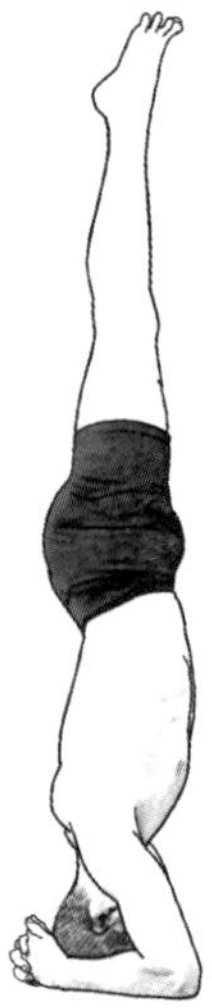

Focus on the vertical mid-line, maintain the actions of the legs and pelvis.

Breathe deeply and evenly.

To learn to balance away from the wall, simply bring one heel slightly away from the wall, then the other. Join your legs. Touch one heel back to the wall whenever needed. Keep your jaw and eyes soft. It is best to build your time in inversions gradually.

specifics of alignment in each category of pose

abdominals

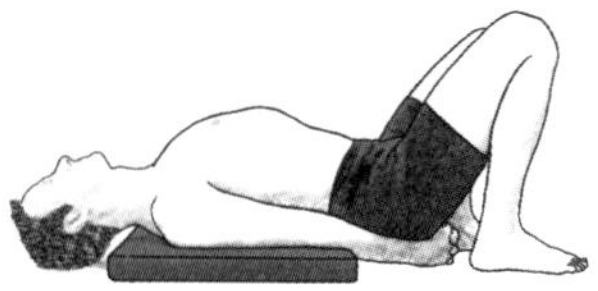
Lengthen side of body and ground the shoulders.

Start rolling the knees over the chest.

Keep the shoulders and wrists grounded.

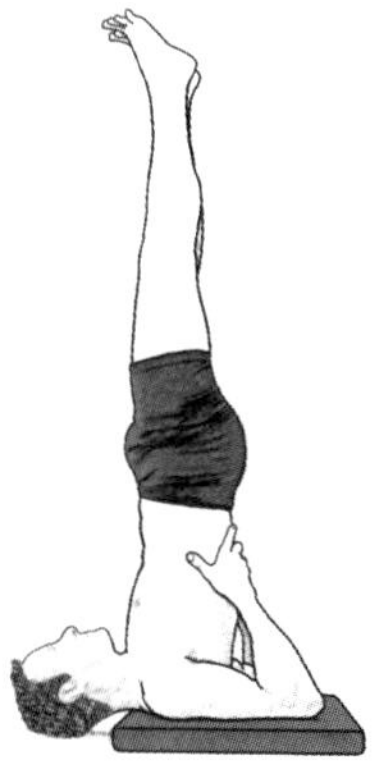
Shoulders press down, legs hug the vertical midline.

Sālamba Sarvāṅgāsana I (Shoulderstand)

Setting the foundation for this inversion is the same as setting up for Setu-Bandha Sarvāṅgāsana (Bridge Building pose; review page 40).

1. While on your back, set shoulders firmly down on your prop. Lengthen the arms and clasp the hands.
2. With knees bent and feet on the floor, draw your knees toward your chest lifting your feet off the floor. Keep your shoulders stationary as your knees continue to draw toward the head.
3. Lift your hips away from the floor as your lower back begins to round.
4. Once your knees are over your face, begin to lengthen your legs, bringing your feet to the floor over your head. This is now Halāsana (Plow pose). With your hips up over your shoulders, legs straight, toes on the floor, place your hands on your back.
5. From this stable position, raise one leg straight up, then the other. Join your legs to the vertical midline. Keep your feet over your hips and your hips over your shoulders.
6. Once you are fully vertical, the actions of the legs and pelvis are the same as for Tāḍāsana. Gaze up at your feet but avoid bringing the feet in line with your eyes, as that can add unnecessary strain on the neck. The feet are over the hips which are over the shoulders.
7. Come down in reverse order. Keep the head and shoulders on the ground. Don't let them pop up.

Note: *I advocate using a prop under your shoulders in Sālamba Sarvāṅgāsana I: a rigid foam pad or a few blankets, 1-2 inches high. This helps maintain a natural curve in the neck and allows for increased mobility of your shoulders, giving you a greater sense of freedom. Without a prop, this pose can flatten your cervical spine, close your throat, and increase strain in your neck and shoulders.*

Abdominals

The waist is the most mobile and often the weakest area of the torso. Āsanas that strengthen the abdominal area are important for developing a strong connection between the upper and lower body. Postures in this category strengthen either the frontal abdominal muscles, the sides of the waist or the deep muscles connecting the upper leg to the pelvis and lower lumbar spine.[7]

The frontal abdominal muscles are responsible for curling the upper torso up away from the floor in a supine position. Ardha Nāvāsana (Half Boat pose) is an example of an āsana that focuses on this area. Jathara Parivartanāsana (Firmly Rotated pose) develops strength in the waist. Ūrdhva Prasārita Pādāsana (Upward Extended Legs pose) and Nāvāsana (Boat pose) develop a powerful connection between the lower limbs and the torso.

For Ardha Nāvāsana (Half Boat Pose):

1. Tuck your tailbone under to make the foundation of the pose the back of your pelvis around the middle of your sacrum.
2. Curl your whole upper body off the floor including your lower back (lumbar region).
3. With legs straight, lift your feet 6-12 inches off the floor using all the principles of the legs and pelvis.

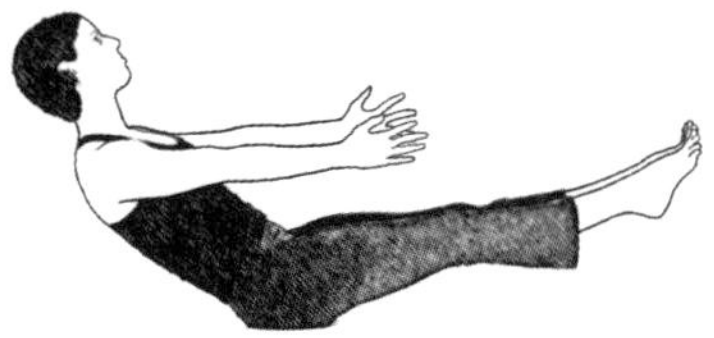
Ardha Nāvāsana

Nāvāsana

In Jathara Parivartanāsana (Firmly Rotated pose), all the principles of the legs and torso are in play:

1. Lying on your back, lengthen the torso and keep your shoulders planted firmly on the floor. Arms out to the side at shoulder height with palms up.
2. Press the legs together, and lengthen the tailbone. Keep a slight lumbar curve throughout.

3. With your legs fully extended, exhale and lower the feet toward your right hand. Pause a few inches above the hand. Inhale return to vertical.
4. Repeat on second side. Build the number of repetitions over time. This pose can also be considered a supine twist, but with the dynamic movement, it is primarily for strengthening the waist.

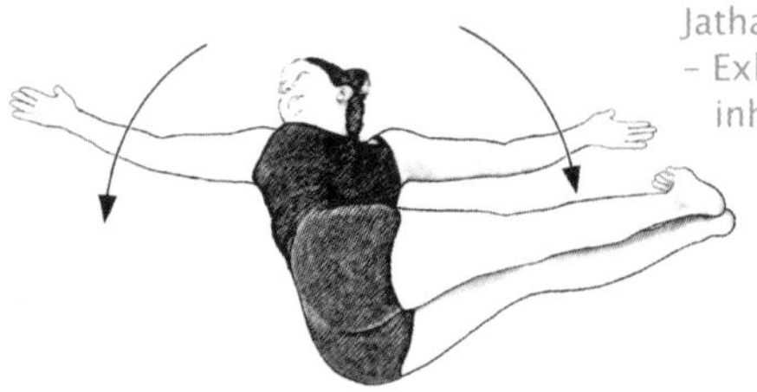

Jathara Parivartanāsana
- Exhale on the way down, inhale on the way up

Ūrdhva Prasārita Pādāsana also utilizes all the principles used in Tāḍāsana. Muscular Engagement of the legs with steady connection to the midline and powerful Energetic Extension are key.

1. Lie on the floor, join the legs. Raise them 45 to 75 degrees, not vertical.
2. Lengthen your tailbone without flattening your lumbar spine. Lower your legs. Don't let your lumbar over arch or your lower ribs jut up away from the floor.
3. Draw the sides of your waist down and keep your lumbar spine lengthened by reaffirming the tailbone.
4. When the legs raise, reaffirm the midline, Energetic Extension, tailbone, and slight curve of the spine. The angle and position of your pelvis and lumbar spine should remain constant as you lower and raise your legs.
5. Avoid clenching your jaw, hardening your throat and chest, or holding your breath. Throughout the movement, extend from your pelvis up through your torso to your hands and from your pelvis down to your feet. Try not to use just your thigh muscles or frontal abdominal muscles (rectus abdominis), as they are less efficient at the action.

Ūrdhva Prasārita Pādāsana
- Exhale on the way down, inhale on the way up

***Note**: Developing awareness of the iliacus and psoas muscles and their connection between the lower body and upper body through the torso is a primary component in developing Mūla Bandha and Uḍḍīyāna Bandha. The underlying physical engagement of these muscles establishes and maintains the energetic flow associated with the bandhas.*

Savasana (Corpse pose)

Śavāsana is the transition between our willful activity in āsana practice and total surrender to what is. This pose gives us time to be completely open and settle deeply into ourselves with absolute presence. Though there is no striving or effort in Śavāsana, we do align the body to promote complete relaxation.

1. Begin by lying on your back with your legs extended about outer hip width apart.
2. Use your hands to widen the flesh of the buttocks away from the midline. This softens the sacrum and lower back.
3. Next move your shoulders slightly up and away from your pelvis and bring your shoulder blades under you, but not pressed together toward the spine. Your upper back should remain spacious. Tip the top of your shoulders down toward the floor so that your collarbones and throat open broadly.
4. Softly place your arms on the floor, palms up, a few inches away from your torso. Keep your head in a neutral position, not tilted back or tucked toward the throat.
5. Observe the natural rhythm of your breath. On your exhale, soften your jaw and throat. Allow your eyes to soften and become still. Allow your belly and lower ribs to soften and naturally descend with gravity. Let your arms and legs completely surrender to the support of the earth. Scan your body for any areas of holding and allow them to soften with the out breath. If thoughts pass through your awareness, allow them to simply drift past like clouds moving through the infinite sky. Allow yourself an inner smile.

Note: I recommend wearing an eye pillow in Śavāsana. It's very soothing. Cover yourself with a blanket to prevent becoming chilled. Try laying a folded blanket across your lap—the slight weight further soothes the nervous system.

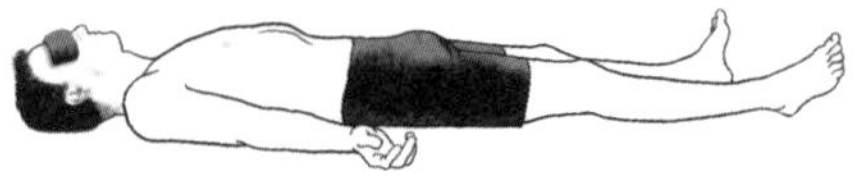

Śavāsana
-Soften your jaw and mouth.
-Soften your eyes.
-Soften your belly.
-Soften your arms and legs.

props and modifications

Modifying a pose or using a prop to make the outer form of a pose more accessible can be very helpful if you have particular physiological limitations such as tight muscles or an injury. The objective is to create stability in a pose and allow for greater range of motion and proper alignment of the limbs and joints. Props may also be used as support so the body may remain in a particular position in proper alignment for an extended period of time. Restorative practice makes extensive use of props in this way.

Many types of props are used in diverse ways for different purposes. The most common prop is a block, often made of dense foam, cork, or wood. Blocks are routinely used under the hand to support the arm and upper body in a variety of standing poses. In Utthita Trikoṇāsana (Extended Triangle pose), for example, using a block under the hand allows you to keep your front leg straight while reducing strain in your hamstrings. As your body opens or the injury heals, you may find you can let go of the prop. Blocks can also be used to help support and stabilize an area of the body to protect the joint and allow a deeper experience of the pose.

Straps or belts help connect a hand to foot, joining the two when the length of our muscles prevents it. Bolsters, blankets, wedge boards, foam rollers, inflated balls and folding chairs are other props that are used in a wide range of applications. Props can help us explore and experiment, create greater accessibility in many poses, and allow us to reap the benefits of yoga āsana practice without compromising proper alignment and safety. With the exception of restorative yoga, props are ultimately a tool for learning the form and alignment of a pose, eventually gaining the proficiency and confidence of doing the poses without them. Since in-depth information on modifications and using props is beyond the scope of the book, I recommend Miriam Austin's *Cool Yoga Tricks* (2003, Random House Publishing Group).

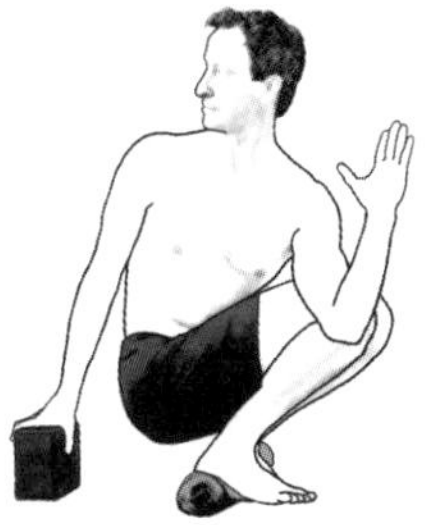
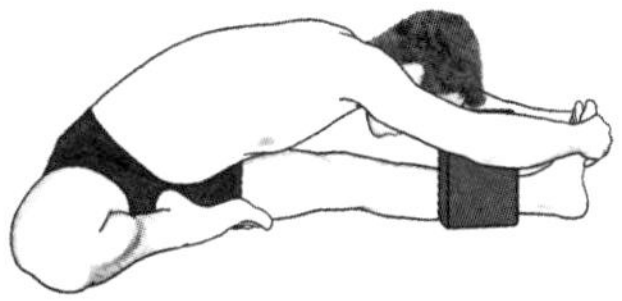

common misalignments

Sometimes, without meaning to, we practice āsana in ways that may not be healthy for our joints and muscles. This is called "misalignment." Until we have an understanding of how the body moves, sometimes we may unconsciously put pressure on our joints or strain on our muscles and ligaments in a way that can lead to injury. I'd like to stress here that practicing yoga postures with attention to alignment isn't just so we can achieve some vision of perfect form, but so that we can ensure that our physical practice creates the opportunity to heal, grow, and find a sense of harmony within.

The following figures illustrate some of the most common misalignments in some of the most basic postures—poses you'll do regularly in nearly any yoga class. If you can become aware of these tendencies, not only will you avoid unnecessary injury, but also the awareness will translate through to all your postures enhancing their effectiveness.

Uttitha Pārśvakoṇāsana

Back leg is bent and passive, pelvis pushed forward. ⊘

Muscular Engagement of the back leg, with emphasis on inward rotation. Tailbone lengthens. Spine extends.

Uttitha Trikoṇāsana

Back leg overly inwardly rotated. No tailbone. Torso unable to turn open. Top arm cranked back. ⊘

Balance of inward rotation of back leg with the tailbone. Spine lengthens, torso turns open, shoulder and arm integrated with core.

Vīrabhadrāsana I

Back foot turn too far out. Back leg becomes too outwardly rotated. Pelvis faces too much to side. ⊘

When back foot angles more to 45 degrees, the back leg gains more inward rotation bringing the pelvis to align forward.

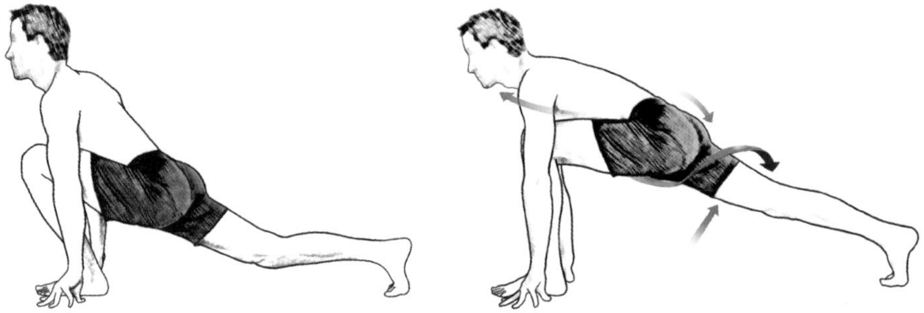

Prakramaṇāsana

Unstable. Front knee bends out past foot. Lack of energy in the rear leg. Pose has diminished extension. ⊘

Front knee over ankle. Rear leg strong and vibrant. Torso extended.

common misalignments

Adho-Mukha Śvanāsana

Results from tight hamstrings. Tailbone overly tucked under, spine and shoulders round up. ⊘

Collapse in the shoulders and and arms can lead to shoulder strain. ⊘

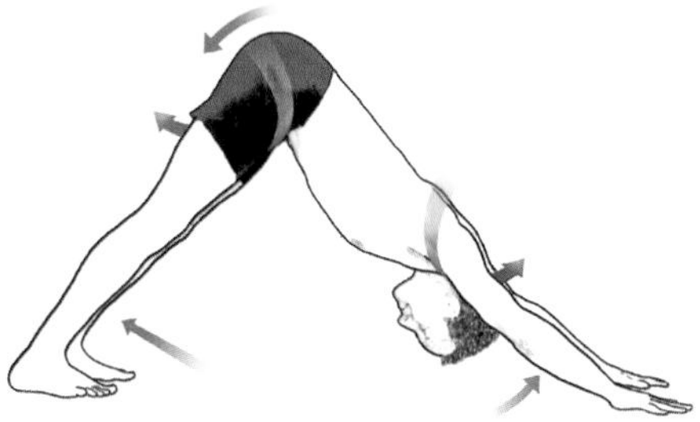

Balanced action in Adho-Mukha Śvanāsana.

Baddha Koṇāsana

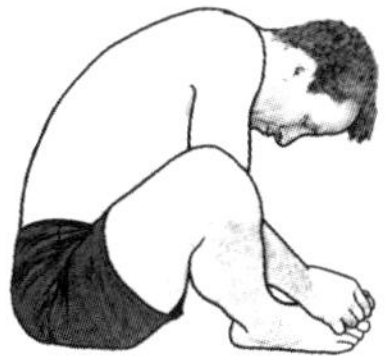

Grabbing the toes and pulling down can tighten the groin while compressing the front body. ⊘

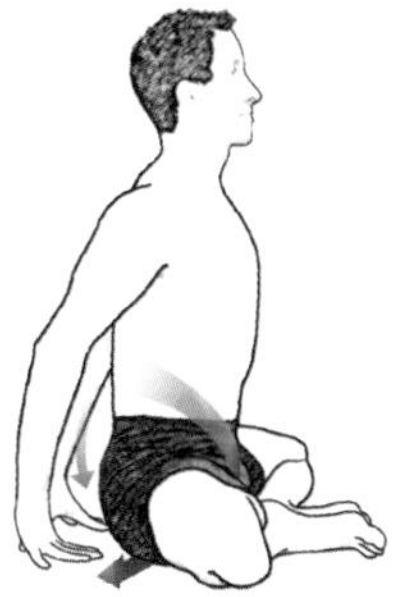

Sitting up with length opens the groins and descends the thighs. Bow forward only when the knees can move to the floor.

Caturaṅga Daṇḍāsana

Hands too far forward and elbows too wide can strain shoulder joint. ⊘

Avoid pressing elbows into waist. ⊘

Proper alignment. Elbows straight back from shoulders, near but not against body.

Shoulders dropping down is a very common misalignment. ⊘

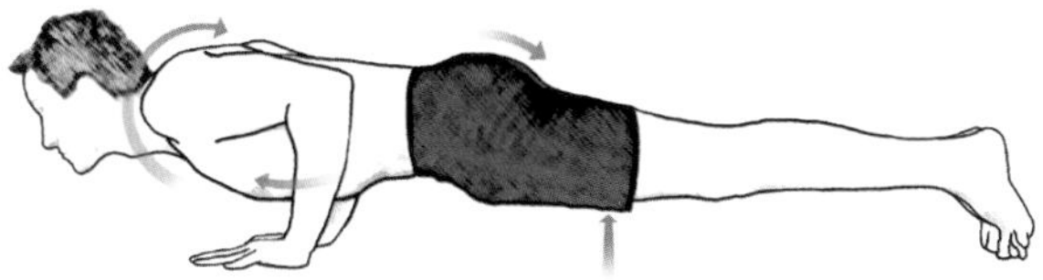

Wrists under elbows, shoulders up away from the floor, tail bone lengthened with firm waist.

Bhujaṅgāsana

Shoulders rolled forward and down. Flattens upper back. ⊘

Arms straight. Body hanging in shoulders. No inner body extension. ⊘

Initiate proper actions of the shoulders, legs and pelvis.

Lengthen and curl the torso. Bring the lower tips of the shoulder blades forward into the heart.

effective yoga sequencing
how to sequence yoga practice

scheduling your home practice

This half of the book details how to design practice sequences that effectively strengthen and integrate your body and mind as well as balance your energy system. It offers a step-by-step, comprehensive method that will help you create yoga sequences to safely and constructively meet your goals.

Scheduling Your Home Practice

Something to consider in creating sequence structures is the time of day you choose to practice. There isn't necessarily a best time for āsana practice, but various times of day will feel different to you. Our energy levels naturally vary during the course of the day. For instance, many of us wake up in the morning feeling more stiff and sluggish than we do as the day progresses. Conversely, at the end of the day we may feel physically and mentally depleted. When we are sensitive to these differences in our energy, we can determine when and how to practice. Of course, work and family obligations will also factor in.

Morning

For many people, life is more quiet and peaceful in the early morning. Responsibilities and demands have not yet begun to mount. We feel fresh and uncluttered. For some, early mornings may offer the only time you have for yourself. A morning āsana practice can be an energizing way to begin the day, bringing balance and poise to all you do. After some dedication to an early morning practice, you may find that morning stiffness dissipates quickly and you can feel just as open and strong as you would at any other time.

Afternoon and Evening

An afternoon or evening practice can be great a way to center and reconnect with yourself within a hectic day. Practicing can help you let go of mental preoccupations and accumulated stress and bring renewed energy to a tired mind and body.

Practicing too strongly or vigorously late at night can make it difficult to sleep. Choose a soothing, slower practice for later in the evening, and keep your focus on the breath. Finish with longer forward folds or an inversion like Vīparita Karani with legs up the wall. This is an ideal preparation for sleep.

Micro Practices

"Micro practices" are short practices that can serve as a break or reset. These shorter intervals of movement and breathing can have an enormously beneficial effect on our physical, mental, and emotional vitality, and on our resiliency. Simple and brief, such practices can be done in a variety of everyday settings without need for special clothes, a yoga mat, or even much space. Some can even be done quite easily at a desk. Examples of micro practices are outlined here on pages 82-83. and in *The Yoga Practice Guide, Volume 2.*

Meals

I won't be talking about diet or what to eat here, just about when to eat. A rule of thumb is to wait 1.5-2 hours after eating before engaging in practice. Practicing *before* your morning, mid-day, or evening meal will feel much more comfortable and is better for digestion.

Energy Rhythms

Our energy levels naturally fluctuate during the day. Our state of mind directly connects to our physical energy level. When we are depressed or just having a hard day, we can feel lethargic, clumsy, drained, and heavy. When our mood is high, we often experience lightness in our body, feel agile, and bubble with enthusiasm and vitality. We may experience the whole gamut of mental and physical energy levels in a single day. Our perception and experience of our outward circumstances play a big part in these fluctuations.

Some people are more lively and enthusiastic the first half of the day, perhaps because of their visit to the coffee shop! Often by afternoon many are beginning to wind down, experiencing both physical and mental fatigue. Some people get a "second wind" later in the evening while others fall into a "couch-lock." Observe your own energy rhythms to decide when the best time for an āsana practice may be. Also consider that a properly sequenced practice can invigorate you when you are fatigued, ground you when you're scattered, and calm you when you feel wired. I share more about sequencing for these specific energy outcomes on page 53. Also refer to *The Yoga Practice Guide, Volume 2.*

Level of Experience

Whether we are designing a personal practice or a sequence for a class, we must make sequences appropriate for the level of the student. We all need to be challenged appropriately for our personal growth and development, but the degree of challenge that can be digested and assimilated will vary from person to person and from day to day. A practical guideline is to compose your sequence using a higher percentage of basic poses, then add in more advanced or complex poses depending on your own or your students' level of experience. Practitioners at any level benefit most from a certain amount of basic or core postures, which can then be built upon.

Class Setting

For teachers, knowing your students is important. That's not always easy when new students or new-to-you students show up to your class. Discerning the level of a student's experience, state of mind, temperament, and energy level can take time. Also, students don't always share information about injuries or other medical conditions, so be sure to make yourself available for such information before class. An effective strategy is to teach to the middle level of the group and offer modifications when possible. These adjustments can be planned ahead when designing a class sequence.

Setting an Intention

Being clear about the purpose or intention of your practice is foundational to determining your sequence. You might be aiming for immediate results such as easing tension in your back and shoulders after sitting at a computer. Having a long-term goal of gaining more range of motion and flexibility in your shoulders and back would involve focusing on those areas over a period of days or months.

Immediate Results

What you need from an āsana practice on any given day will vary. How you sequence your practice will impact how you feel afterwards. For example, at the end of a hectic day, a gentle restorative sequence might offer more balance and rest than a vigorous vinyāsa practice. Or, a vinyāsa sequence might be just what you need to lift you out of lethargy and invigorate you. You can also address muscle tightness or range of motion with your sequence, using certain poses to open specific areas of the body.

Long-term Results

Developing strength and flexibility in the body is a longer-term process. A methodically designed sequence will help you focus on a specific intention or goal such as opening the hips or lengthening the hamstrings. The variety of sequences for opening any area of the body is virtually limitless.

sequencing basics

creating a foundational sequence

Creating a Foundational Sequence

Choose a few poses from each category appropriate to your level and experience (see categories on pages 92-103). Practice this basic sequence for a while. When you feel ready, expand upon your area of chosen focus. This added emphasis could be done a few ways. At first, you would practice your foundational sequence over a few days or weeks. As you gain experience in the initial poses and these poses have become easier and more familiar, replace some of the poses with more challenging versions. This gradual process of deepening the initial poses within a routine then adding additional poses to expand the scope of the routine is very effective. It is a methodical way to progress and minimize any risk of injury. It also allows you to clearly see your progress since you're working with the same few poses over several practice sessions.

Creating Multiple Sequences

Another method is to design two or three slightly different sequences, each with the same focus or emphasis, such as hip openers or standing balances. Designing more than one sequence will take a little more time and creativity, but will keep your practice sessions from feeling repetitive.

Weekly Practice Plan

An effective way to practice is to concentrate on a certain area of the body or on a certain energy-balancing result. You can have different concentrations for each day of the week, while still covering a variety of poses within a full spectrum sequence.

For example:
Monday - hip openers
Tuesday - twists and forward folds
Wednesday - arm balances
Thursday - backbends
Friday - inversions.

Add a day of restorative practice[8], and you have a very well-balanced weekly routine applicable to either a class or personal home practice.

> *"In freeing the body we free the heart to experience the power of love."*
>
> ~ Gabrielle Roth—
> *Maps to Ecstasy, The Healing Power of Movement*

Longer-term Sequence Plans

A week-long sequence plan like the one just outlined may be part of a more extended plan of development spanning several months. Staying with the concept of a particular emphasis for each day of the week, you can progress each daily routine over time.

1. Within each of your daily sequences, start with basic poses. When you feel confident, add a deeper pose within that category. For example, a backbend sequence, may initially include two basic backbends. Over several weeks, while most of the initial sequence remains the same, you'd work up to four or five backbends, or variations on the original two.
2. Another approach to a longer-term course of practice is to focus on a specific area of the body such as the hips and pelvis over a period of a week or more. Each practice that week would focus on the same general area. With this approach you can really explore and refine your understanding of a particular area of the body and create a shift in openness or flexibility more quickly and deeply because of the sustained focus.

general sequencing guidelines
beginning

I'll outline here the various components and possibilities for designing effective sequences. Any type or style of practice will have a beginning, middle, and end. The beginning section of a sequence should have a short, seated centering element. Next would come a brief section of simple movement as part of a "warm-up." The warm-up can progress to stronger poses that recruit the larger muscles of the body. Next would be a series of standing poses to further raise heat and stamina. Following standing poses would come a series of more demanding poses. A cool down follows with poses designed to bring down heart rate and respiration and have a soothing effect overall. Final relaxation is the end of any sequence where you totally relax and surrender the body and mind in a supported, effortless posture, usually Śavāsana.

The cycles of nature and the seasons are a perfect metaphor for sequence building. We start quiet and still in a seated posture at the beginning of our practice, just as Winter is poised for Spring. The gradual warm awakening of Spring transitions into the bright, full exuberance of Summer. The power of Summer peaks, then moves toward the descending energy of Autumn. Autumn folds inward, finally releasing back to Winter and its silence. When designing your own sequencing, keep the rhythm of the seasons in mind.

Beginning

Seated Centering
In any āsana practice, whether at home or in a class, a short seated centering at the beginning will help bring focus to your practice. Bring attention to the rhythm of the breath. This helps you attune to your body and allows thoughts and preoccupations to subside. Notice any areas of tension and let them soften and release on the exhalation. Include an uplifting contemplation that connects to your heart, setting the tone and mood of your practice. Choose a word, phrase, or image that allows you to better recognize the blessing and wonder of your own life.

Warm-up
No matter your experience level (or that of your class), keep the initial warm-up simple. Whether you are teaching a class or practicing at home, anyone's body will benefit from a slower, uncomplicated series of basic movements.

A fancy or challenging warm-up isn't necessary even if you're teaching seasoned students or are a seasoned practitioner yourself. To start any practice, do slow, simple, repetitive movements combined with full rhythmic breathing. Aim to connect movement and breath, gently raise the heart rate, oxygenate the blood and lubricate the joints[9]. Include some weight bearing poses to get the major muscles of the body working. These poses should not require a lot of instruction nor should they put much strain on muscles and joints. Prakramaṇāsana (Lunge pose) is a good example of a steady pose that is relatively easy to perform yet demands enough engagement to get the heart pumping. Simple basic poses warm up the bigger muscle groups and help us get out of our head and into our body.

For home practitioners, the beauty of practicing at home is you are able to check in with how you feel and proceed accordingly rather than keep up with someone else's agenda. This gives you the freedom to begin your practice in a way that feels best to your body on any given day.

Middle

Usually the middle section of any sequence, no matter what style or approach, demands the most of us. The postures in this section raise the heart rate, build heat in the body, require mental focus, encourage deeper respiration, and often stimulate the nervous system in an elevating way. These earlier more vigorous poses also tone and balance the endocrine, lymphatic, and metabolic systems, as well as the internal energy system of the body.

End

Cool Down
This is an essential aspect of any sequence plan. The cool down is where we shift from more dynamic poses to a state of surrender and relaxation. Most poses in this section of a sequence are poses done on the floor, held for longer duration and with slow, full, even breath. It's a place to deeply open the body and transition to a more internal perspective.

Final Relaxation

The final pose of any sequence allows for total release and relaxation. This last stage of āsana practice gives space for all the systems of the body to settle and reintegrate. The mind can become completely passive with no other agenda or task. We give ourselves permission to simply do nothing yet be blissfully present.

types of practice
sequencing for "peak poses"

Sequencing for "Peak Poses"

A "peak pose" is the most difficult or deepest pose planned for your practice. This means you'll need to prepare your body in the earlier part of the sequence for your planned peak pose. You'll use earlier poses to emphasize areas of the body relevant to the peak pose. For example, if you have selected a deep backbend as your peak pose, you would include movements and basic postures that warm up the shoulders and upper back as well as the front of the body. When you get to the actual backbend segment of your planned sequence, you would lead with simpler backbends before performing the peak pose backbend.

Energy Balancing Sequences

With this approach, you create sequences of poses to affect and balance your energy levels. Depending on your tendencies or simply on what kind of day you are having, you may want either a Grounding, Calming, or Invigorating practice.[10] These three categories address physical, mental, and emotional states likely common to all of us. Each type of practice is designed to help bring us back into balance when our state of mind, mood, or life situation has us feeling less than our radiant best.

Grounding Sequences

Sequences of this type build strength and demand focus. They help re-direct nervous energy and develop physical stamina while settling the mind. If you have a quick, creative mind but tend to be a bit unfocused in your attention, or are athletic but often feel a bit scattered, practicing in a way that brings more grounding will be of great benefit.

These sequences should meet you where you are and begin with movement. They then progress to standing poses, which demand strong use of your legs and hips, anchoring you to the earth. Practice them with longer holds and deep, full breathing. The muscular engagement required to stay in longer holds will bring you fully into your body, settling your mind and insulating your nervous system. You'll then move to the floor for powerful arm balances, twists, and forward folds, all of which should be done with the same full, smooth breath and long holds. The underlying idea for any Grounding practice is to begin with movement, then progress to stillness, just as mountains quell the blowing wind. In Śavāsana, release the arms and legs heavily onto the earth.

Calming Sequences

Perhaps you are active and willful, always rising to a challenge. Maybe you tend to push hard and overwork, creating strain or agitation in your body and mind. The Calming practices should be done slowly and methodically to temper these fiery tendencies. Try not to overwork in this practice. Movement should be done in a fluid way, with smooth and relaxed breathing, avoiding any aggressive approach. These fire-tempering sequences move to the floor early on, bringing you into connection with the elements of water and earth. Hip openers bring you further into the earth energy of the body and should be given ample time. Do twists without over-efforting and keep the breath calm and flowing. Relax and settle deeply into your Śavāsana softening the eyes, throat, and belly.

Invigorating Sequences

These are strong, dynamic practices to help build heat and will, balancing any tendency toward inactivity or feelings of lethargy. Sequences begin with simple movement and full breathing, then shift to more vigorous standing poses. Movement, reflecting the air element, is key here. Practice the postures with power and strength and work to maintain a continuous flow. Arm balances keep the fire building, fanned by robust breath. Go deeply into twists and forward folds then come out and repeat them again rather than staying in these typically cooling postures for long periods. A brief Śavāsana keeps the energy bright and the body warm.

***Note**: It's important not to judge ourselves for our tendencies but simply to recognize them. When we are able objectively see where we are we can then determine the most appropriate course of action.*

**My book,* The Yoga Practice Guide, Volume 2*, features several sequencing examples and provides ample information on how your practice can positively influence your energy levels and state of mind.*

vinyasa/flow practice

home vinyasa sequencing

Practicing a smooth, uninterrupted flow of postures can produce a delightful sense of freedom and exuberance. Sequencing vinyāsa flow can be a very creative process, something like choreographing dance. This style of practice emphasizes logical and smooth transitions to create a continuous flow of postures and breath. Generally poses in vinyāsa flow are not held for longer than twenty to thirty seconds. As in all types of āsana practice, keeping a very close connection between the rhythm of breath and the movement of the body is an important key feature here. Ideally the breath is long, deep, and smooth, and the movement of the body follows in tandem with it. The consistent synchronicity of movement and breath allows prāṇa to flow in the body and helps produce a meditative state of mind within the demands of the physical practice.

The foundation of vinyāsa flow sequences is the Sūrya Namaskāra (Sun Salutation). This set of postures repeats often within the routine. The various forms of Flow, Power, or Vinyāsa yoga are a relatively fast-paced practice incorporating a spectrum of foundational poses joined together through the Sūrya Namaskāra base.[11] Vinyāsa or flow practice can be fun and creative. It also requires some knowledge and training to experience the joy of movement while staying safe in the body. This form of practice is often the first exposure many students have to yoga.

I recommend balancing vinyāsa style practice with slower, more methodical alignment-based practice occasionally. Theresa Elliot is a talented yoga teacher whose display of strength, poise, and grace in her video, Stillness in Motion, is unparalleled. Elliot says that for every one vinyāsa style practice, she does five slower, more alignment-based practices working on the fundamentals of each pose. She spends the time to understand the connection between technique, movement, and breath. I agree with this approach. The benefits of taking time to really develop a foundation in technique will spare you confusion, discouragement, and potential injury down the road.

Home Vinyasa Sequencing

To develop your own vinyāsa sequences, get on your mat and experiment. See what spontaneously occurs to you. Write down sequences that feel good to you. Keep a library of these notes to draw on for the future. Combining sections from various sequences you've developed in your own practice sessions can offer an almost endless repertoire to draw from and recombine.

Teaching Vinyasa Sequences

If you are a teacher, categorize sequences or segments of whole routines into beginner, intermediate, and advanced levels. You can also start with a beginner sequence and then embellish it by adding more advanced aspects to create a higher level or more challenging version of the same basic sequence. You essentially use the same "base" sequence and then create variations of it.

Be prudent when bringing sequences to a class that you have created for your own practice. Make sure the sequence is appropriate for the level of student you are working with. You can challenge students without discouraging them with an overly complex or difficult sequence. Test out any sequence first in your own practice before teaching it in class to familiarize yourself with it and work out the details.

Note: Avoid rushing your movement to catch up with your breath or rushing your breath to catch up to your movement. If you find this is happening, give room to pause and reconnect. Adho-Mukha Śvanāsana (Downward Facing Dog pose) is ideal for this.

Standing Poses

Standing poses heat up the entire body by stimulating the large muscles of the legs. While building strength and stamina, they develop balance, confidence, and mental alertness. They encourage prāṇic expansion and extension in the upper body and spine and help open the hips and shoulders.

Standing sequences follow the warm-up. No matter how experienced a student is, the first few standing poses should be simple. Basic standing poses include any pose where both feet are on the ground and there are no twists or strong demands on balance. Poses that require balancing on one leg, such as Ardha-Candrāsana (Half-Moon pose) or Vṛkṣāsana (Tree pose), as well as revolved standing poses, should come later into a standing sequence. Since these poses require greater mental focus, introducing them later into a practice allows students time to "arrive" in their bodies, clear their minds, and establish their breath. Introduce one pose at a time to beginning students. More advanced students can combine a series of two or three poses sequenced together. (See Standing Pose series, pages 65-69).

Ardha-Candrāsana

Vṛkṣāsana

Forward Folds

Standing Forward Folds

Standing forward folds such as Uttānāsana are considered standing poses and can be incorporated into an initial standing sequence as a way to begin to warm the body and open the hamstrings along with the entire back of the body. Begin modestly with the first few introduced into a standing sequence. As the body warms, go deeper in your poses.

Uttānāsana

Seated Forward Folds

Bring forward folds into a sequence after the body has had time to build heat. Where they appear in a sequence will depend on your overall objective. For example, after a working the legs and sufficiently warming up the body in standing poses, you might move to the floor for one or two seated forward folds. This can bring focus to the hamstrings and help open the legs and lower back for certain arm balances such as Ṭiṭṭibhāsana (Firefly pose). Generally forward folds help cool the body. They are done on the floor with relatively little movement, slowing down the heart rate and other physical processes. Forward folds have a settling, introspective effect on the mind. From this perspective, seated forward folds are best introduced in the later part of a sequence as part of the cool down.

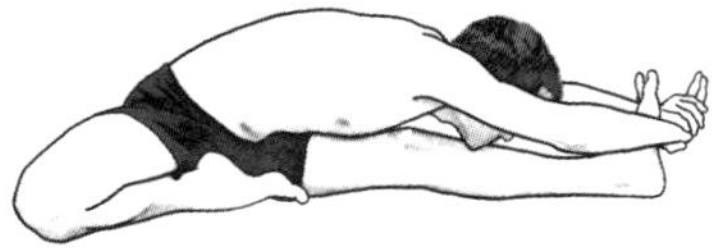

Jānu-Śīrṣāsana

Ṭiṭṭibhāsana

Forward Folds as Counter Poses

A counter pose opens or lengthens an area of the body where the muscles have been contracted and shorted from an earlier pose. Because backbends contract the muscles of the back, buttocks and hips, forward folds after backbends are ideal to help open these areas.

Hip Openers

Basic hip openers such as Baddha-Koṇāsana (Bound Angle pose), Agnistambhāsana (Fire-log pose), and Eka-Pāda Rājakapotāsana I preparation (One Leg King Pigeon II - aka "Pigeon") help prepare the body for deeper hip openers such as Padmāsana (Lotus pose) or Eka-Pāda Śīrṣāsana (Leg Behind the Head pose). They also help greatly in arm balances, many of which require open hips. Opening the hips also helps open the lower back in preparation for backbends. Some advanced inversions also include Padmāsana. By opening the hips we facilitate the flow of prāṇa throughout the body. Hip opening poses particularly enhance the prāṇic connection of the lower body with the upper body. Freeing the flow of prāṇa creates more power, stability, extension, and ease in all yoga poses.

Baddha Koṇāsana

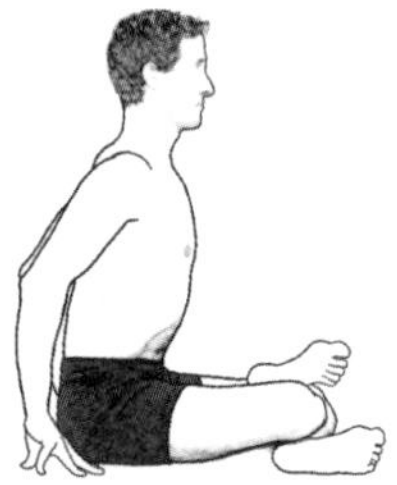

Agnistambhāsana

Eka-Pāda Rājakapotāsana I preparation (aka "Pigeon")

Abdominals

Sometimes the abdominal region gets overlooked in sequencing. While strengthening the rectus abdominis (the "six pack") is helpful, the deeper muscles of the psoas that connect the legs to the inside of the pelvis and lower spine are of primary importance in āsana practice (see page 10). Creating awareness of and consciously toning these muscles brings tremendous stability, strength, and lightness to the body. Poses that directly strengthen the psoas are Nāvāsana (Boat pose) Ūrdhva Prasārita Padāsana (Supine Leg Lifts) and Vṛṣapāda-Kṣepāsana (Kicking the Bull pose). You can add these poses almost anywhere in a practice sequence.

Adding these poses early in the sequence helps connect our mind to our abdominal area, awakening Mūla Bandha and Uḍḍīyāna Bandha. Since most abdominal poses are floor poses, if you are doing a vinyāsa format you might save them for later when you are approaching hip openers, twists, and forward folds. Abdominal poses are heating and require stamina, so don't put them at the very end of your routine.

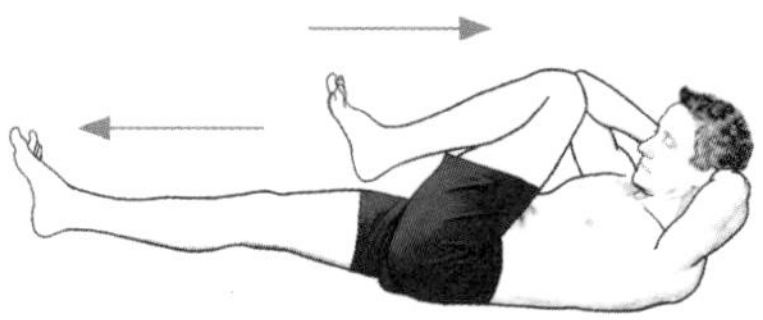

Vṛṣapāda-Kṣepāsana

Nāvāsana

Ūrdhva Prasārita Pādāsana

Twists and Revolved Poses

All twisted or revolved poses open the muscles of lower back and waist, and to a lesser degree, the outer hips. Twists encourage fluid exchange and blood flow to all muscles and tissues around the spine and have a cleansing and balancing effect on the internal organs and glands. Along with hip openers they have a profoundly positive effect on prāṇic flow in the body.

There are three basic types of twists:

1. Seated revolved poses, such as Mārīcyāsana III (Mārīci's pose).
2. Supine revolved poses, such as Parivṛtta Supta Pādānguṣṭhāsana (Revolved Reclined Hand to Big Toe pose).
3. Standing revolved poses, such as Parivṛtta Pārśvakoṇāsana (Revolved Side Angle pose), a standing pose category.

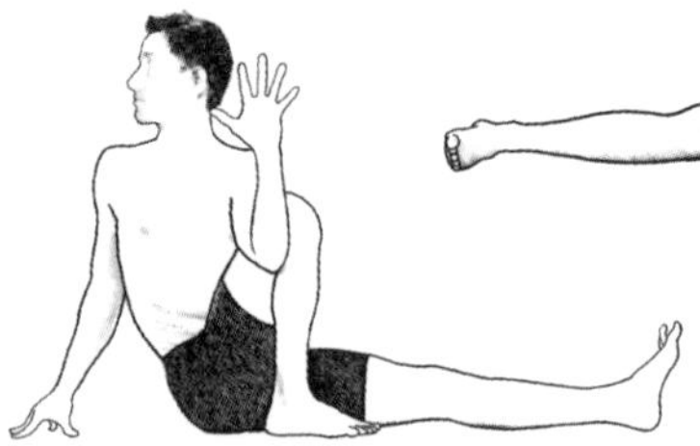

Mārīcyāsana III

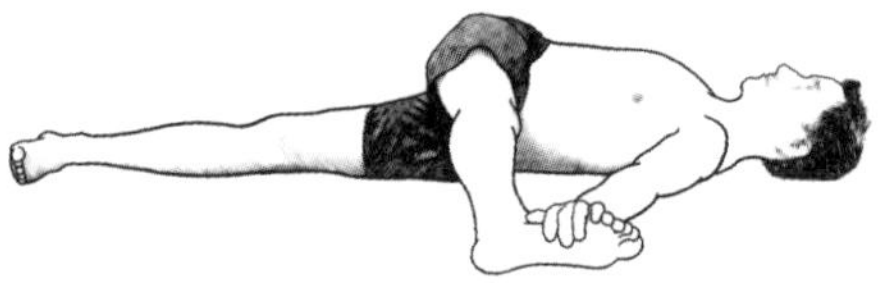

Parivṛtta Supta Pādānguṣṭhāsana

Parivṛtta Pārśvakoṇāsana

Practicing seated twists prior to backbending helps bring flexibility to the lower spine and hips. Focusing on the inhalation adds a subtle energizing effect. Used after backbends, twists open muscles of the hips and back that have been strongly contracted during backbends. Focusing on the exhalation brings a calming, neutralizing affect.

Standing revolved poses work the same areas as seated twists. They generally require the body to be well warmed up so add standing revolved poses to a sequence only after other more basic standing poses. Revolved standing poses require strong mental focus and develop balance and stamina.

Arm Balances

Arm balances build courage, will, and confidence. They require significant strength and can be tremendously exhilarating. Arm balances should be introduced within the first half of a sequence while students still have plenty of energy. Depending on which arm balances you include, it can be helpful to lead with revolved standing poses and some basic shoulder, and hip openers. Opening these areas first will help you access arm balances more deeply. The more open the body is first, the less effort arm balances require.

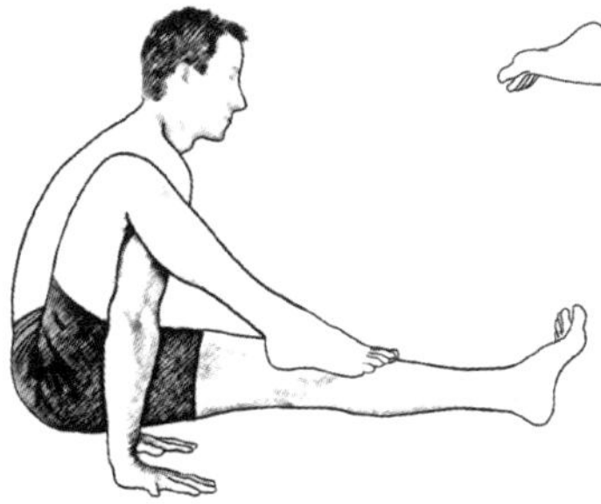

Eka-Pāda Bhujāsana

Eka-Pāda Bakāsana I

Thigh Stretches

Because of their size and strength, thigh muscles are often tight. The psoas, which can be considered a leg muscle for our purposes, is often short and tight from prolonged sitting during our everyday life. For this reason, it is good to incorporate some form of thigh opening in a sequence regardless of whether backbends will follow. As part of a standing sequence, poses like Sañcalanāśvāsana (Low Lunge) and Āñjaneyāsana (Añjaneya's pose) both begin to open your thighs, groins, and front of your body.

Poses such as Eka-Pāda Rājakapotāsana I preparation (aka "Pigeon"), Vīrāsana (Hero pose), or Supta Vīrāsana (Reclining Hero pose) open the thighs and psoas in preparation for backbends. They should be held for 30 seconds or more to allow the body to release. When these areas are opened, the spine can bend more easily and evenly. Compression in the sacrum, and lower back during backbends is significantly reduced.

Sañcalanāśvāsana

Āñjaneyāsana

Vīrāsana

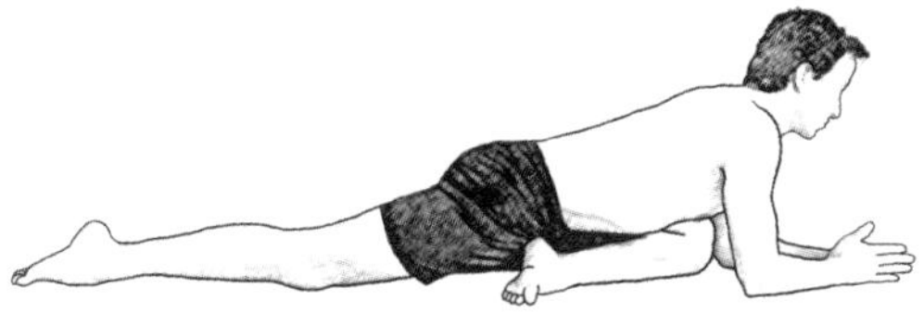

Eka-Pāda Rājakapotāsana I Prep (aka "Pigeon")

Supta Vīrāsana

Backbends

Backbends range in intensity from moderate to very intense. Deep backbends should be considered a peak pose in a sequence and should not be brought in sooner than half way through the practice. Advanced backbends are relatively complex poses and require a great deal of strength and stamina. They stimulate strong prāṇic flow throughout the body and are expansive and heart opening in nature.

Before backbending, make sure the whole body is very warmed up and open, particularly the shoulders, lower back, pelvic floor, groins, and front of the thighs. Include Bhujaṅgāsana (Cobra pose) as a key part of the warm-up. Also bring focus to the shoulders and upper back in standing poses. Begin the backbend segment of your sequence with less challenging backbends such as basic Śalabhāsana (Locust pose), Setu-Bandha Sarvāṅgāsana (Bridge Building pose), and Dhanurāsana (Bow pose), then progress to deeper poses.

Bhujaṅgāsana

Śalabhāsana

Adho-Mukha Vṛkṣāsana

Piñca Mayūrāsana

Setu-Bandha Sarvāṅgāsana

Dhanurāsana

Ūrdhva Dhanurāsana

Vīparita Daṇḍāsana

Practicing Ūrdhva Hastāsana (Handstand) earlier in the sequence prepares for the work in the arms and shoulders needed in Ūrdhva Dhanurāsana (Upward Bow pose) and its variations. Piñca Mayūrāsana (Peacock Tail pose) done in the first half of a sequence informs the upper back and shoulders for all Vīparita Daṇḍāsana (Inverted Staff pose) and its variations.

Because of their stimulating nature, backbends require ample cool-down time. Never end a sequence with backbends. Instead use, twists, and forward folds as counter or finishing postures. These lengthen, soften, and relax the back muscles and will help soothe the nervous system.

Inversions - Headstand/Shoulderstand

Inversions have both physical and energetic benefits. Physically elevating the legs cleanses toxins from the body by encouraging drainage of the lymphatic system.[12] Inverting also has a regulating effect on blood pressure by stimulating the vagus nerve in the neck.[13] It also allows blood to flow away from the lower limbs and takes downward pressure off ligaments that hold the internal organs in place.

Traditional yoga presents inversions as a method to spiritual attainment. By inverting the body, it was believed you could reverse Apāṇa vāyu, the downward flowing prāṇic energy current. From this perspective the aim of inversions is to encourage as much prāṇa to move from the base of the spine, through the central channel of the body (Suṣumṇā Nāḍi), to the crown of the head. It was thought that moving both Prāṇa vāyu (the upward prāṇic current) and Apāṇa vāyu (downward current) upward led to a clearing of the main spiritual channel thereby making complete spiritual transformation attainable (see Prāṇa Vāyus on page 32).

pose categories

inversions

Sālamba Śīrṣāsana (Headstand)
Sālamba Śīrṣāsana I and all other headstands are considered heating poses, particularly when including various leg and arm variations. Once Sālamba Śīrṣāsana I is mastered, it can be very soothing and meditative if held for just 2 to 5 minutes. Held longer (up to 10 minutes), it becomes more strenuous and heating.

Sālamba Śīrṣāsana I is the foundation to all other headstand variations. Take your time learning this pose. Start with short headstands and progress to longer holds. Leg and arm variations should only be introduced once Sālamba Śīrṣāsana I can be comfortably maintained for 5 to 10 minutes away from the wall. Sālamba Śīrṣāsana II is used primarily as a transition pose to other hand variations. It typically requires more work in the shoulders so is not ideal for extended holds.

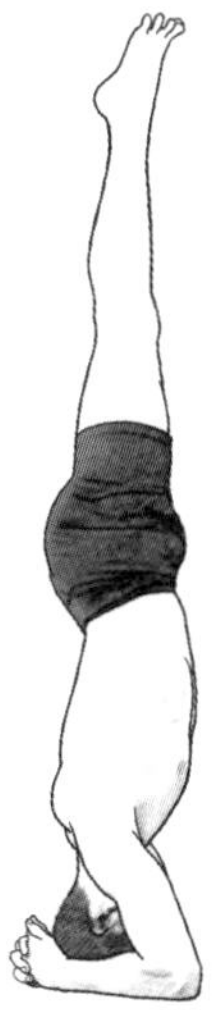

Sālamba Śīrṣāsana I

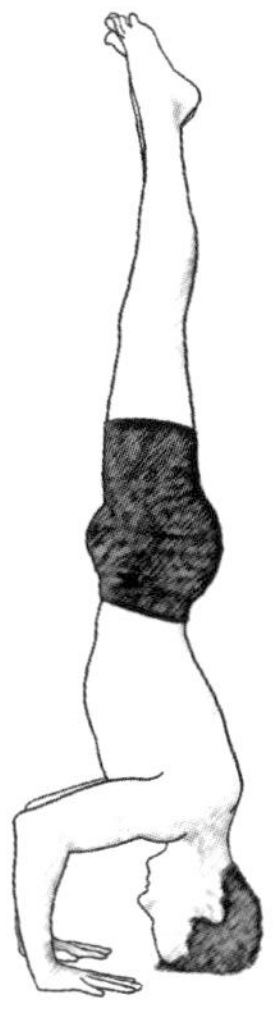

Sālamba Śīrṣāsana II

Sālamba Sarvāṅgāsana (Shoulderstand)
Sālamba Sarvāṅgāsana I is the complement to headstand and usually follows headstands. Make sure your shoulders, chest, and upper back are warm and open before doing this pose. Considered a cooling posture, it is a good counter pose for deep backbends. Sālamba Sarvāṅgāsana I is a relatively advanced pose that requires open shoulders. Free standing Vīparita Karaṇi, or "legs up the wall," has the same benefits as Sālamba Sarvāṅgāsana and can be more restful and more easily accessed by beginning students.

Vīparita Karaṇi

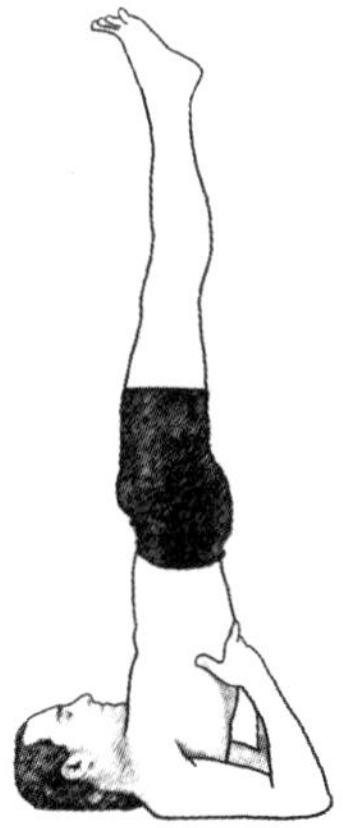

Sālamba Sarvāṅgāsana I

Setu-Bandha Sarvāṅgāsana

Whether backbends are part of your sequence or not, preceding Sālamba Sarvāṅgāsana I with Setu-Bandha Sarvāṅgāsana (Bridge Building pose) informs the shoulders for this inversion.

Halāsana (Plow)
Once in Sālamba Sarvāṅgāsana I, Halāsana can be used as a resting pose. This pose is also a good place to adjust and realign the shoulders to then return back up to Sālamba Sarvāṅgāsana I. Halāsana opens the whole back of the body and further opens the shoulders. It is a grounding pose and soothing on the nervous system. From this perspective it can be included in both grounding and calming sequences. For the same reason it should be placed toward the end of most any sequence as part of the cool down or finishing poses. It can be used for this purpose on its own without headstand or shoulderstand preceding it.

Halāsana

***Note**: There are a few precautions for inversions. Generally, inversions are not recommended if you have any issues with your eyes, inner ears, sinuses, or neck. Women who are menstruating might consider waiting until after their cycle to engage in inversions as inversions may interrupt the natural flow. Vīparita Karaṇi (legs up the wall version) is a good alternative after the first two or three days of bleeding. Inversions can be continued during pregnancy if you already have an established practice and there are no health concerns. Seek advice from your health provider and an experienced yoga teacher regarding any of these before engaging in inversions.*

pose categories
cool down and finishing poses

Cool Down or Finishing Poses

Cooling down is an important aspect of any sequence. Transitioning from more vigorous poses to a state of total surrender and relaxation, as in Śavāsana (Corpse pose), is just as important as moving through a warm-up.

The entire body and all its systems are stimulated during the first half of a soundly designed āsana sequence. The second half of a sequence devotes time and attention to reintegration. The cool down or finishing postures help bring the heart rate and breathing down to the slower rhythm of rest. Winding down our practice means decreasing the demand on the structure of the body. In the cool down process, the nervous system shifts its work to the parasympathetic system as the body slows and quiets down. The blood pressure naturally lowers. Blood vessels in the tissues that have been engorged begin to reduce, and capillaries shrink dramatically.[14] As body temperatures decreases, the cool down allows all the body's processes to return to integration and equilibrium.

What you incorporate into a cool down sequence depends in part on which poses you did during the practice, how vigorous the practice was, and both your energy level and state of mind when you began the practice. A general guideline for any cool down is to move to floor poses, focusing on forward folds and supine twists. Stay 30 to 60 seconds in each side of a twist without strain. Cultivate an even, slow breath emphasizing the exhale. Always finish your practice with a Śavāsana for 5 to 15 minutes. The deepest balancing and integration of both the body and mind takes place in this final relaxation pose.

Cool Down for Backbends

Backbends tend to be rather vigorous, strong poses for most people. They require strength, stamina and mental focus. The aim of a cool down is to restore balance to the muscles around the spine and hips and settle the nervous system.

The back or posterior part of the vertebral discs and muscles surrounding the spine have received more compression during backbends while the anterior or front of the spine has been stretched more open. Energetically, backbends are considered an "extroverted" pose, opening up the body's energy. Balance this with the more "introverted" forward folds, to bring the body's energy down and initiate a more meditative state. Mild seated or supine twists and forward folds help bring balance to the tissues of the spine, particularly the lower back and sacral area. In the case of a practice that has focused on backbends, incorporating gentle seated hip openers as part of the cool down will also help to release the outer hips and sacrum.

Example:

1. Lie on your back and lightly hold your bent knees to your chest, Urasyubhayajānvāsana (Both Knees to Chest pose)
2. Transition to a supine twist such as Parivṛtta Supta Pādānguṣṭhāsana (Revolved Reclined Big Toe pose)
3. Supine hip opener such as Sūcīrandhrāsana (Eye of the Needle pose)
4. Next move to Gomukhāsana (Cow's Mouth pose)
5. Agnistambhāsana (Fire Logs pose)
6. Paścimottānāsana (Back Stretched Out pose)

Urasyubhayajānvāsana

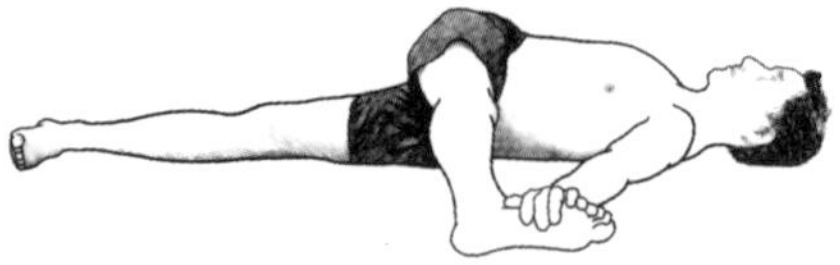
Parivṛtta Supta Pādānguṣṭhāsana

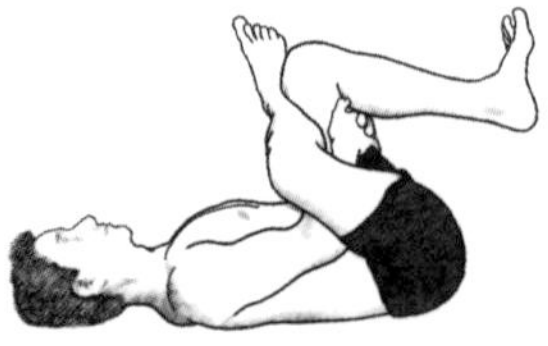
Sūcīrandhrāsana

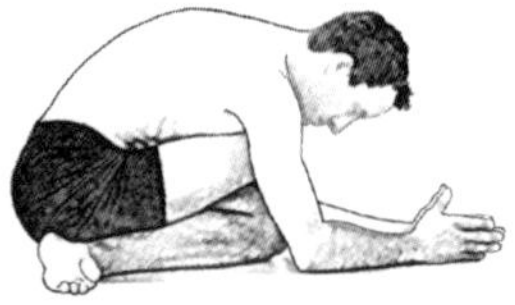
Gomukhāsana

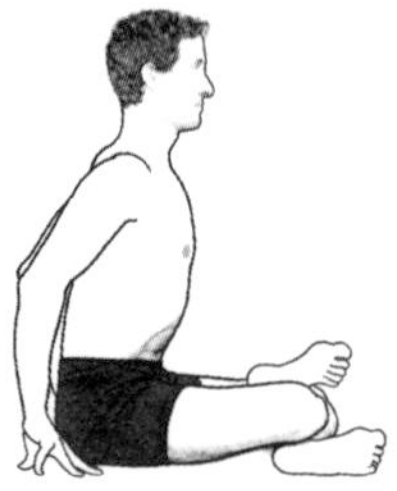
Agnistambhāsana

Paścimottānāsana

Savasana — Final Resting Pose

Sequences can be concluded with quiet sitting for several minutes, but lying still and relaxed in Śavāsana (Corpse pose) allows for more complete rest and surrender. Aligning the body in Śavāsana supports this process.

How to Align Śavāsana

1. Lie on your back with your feet at least outer hip width apart.
2. Widen the buttocks away from the midline with your hands.
3. Place your arms at your sides a comfortable distance away from the body, palms facing up.
4. Lengthen the torso up away from the hips and bring the shoulder blades gently under you.
5. The neck has a natural curve and the chin is neutral. Avoid drawing the chin into the throat or lifting it up with the head tilted back.
6. Soften the eyes, throat, belly and limbs.

Śavāsana

sequence components
seated centering

We'll now look at each sequencing component, or section, and break it down step by step.

Seated Centering

Choose a seated posture that is easy to maintain for 5 minutes or more. I recommend Sukhāsana (Easy pose), Muktāsana (Pose of Liberation) or Siddhāsana (Perfected One's pose). Sit on the edge of a folded blanket, so your knees rest slightly lower than the crest of your pelvis. This allows the weight of your body to be squarely on your sit bones. Close your eyes. Gently lengthen the sides of your body and spine upward. Lift and expand your chest bringing your shoulders up and back. Soften your arms, belly, and legs. Feel the movement in your lower belly as the breath moves in and out. Notice your breath passing in and out of the nostrils. The hands can rest palms down on the thighs or can be placed in a specific mudrā. (See The Yoga Practice Guide, Volume 2 for mudrās and their function.)

Sukhāsana

Muktāsana

Siddhāsana

Warm-Up

For many people, especially beginning yoga students, sitting on the floor can get uncomfortable after a few minutes, so come to standing after centering. Initiate simple movements that can easily be coordinated with the breath.

Warm-up Example 1 — Beginner

1. Standing at the front of your mat, raise your arms over head on the inhalation and lower them with the exhalation.
2. Uttānāsana (Standing Forward Fold). Bend and straighten the legs several times with hands on knees or on floor.
3. From standing, transition to Adho-Mukha Śvanāsana (Downward Facing Dog pose).
4. Step to Prakramaṇāsana (Lunge pose).

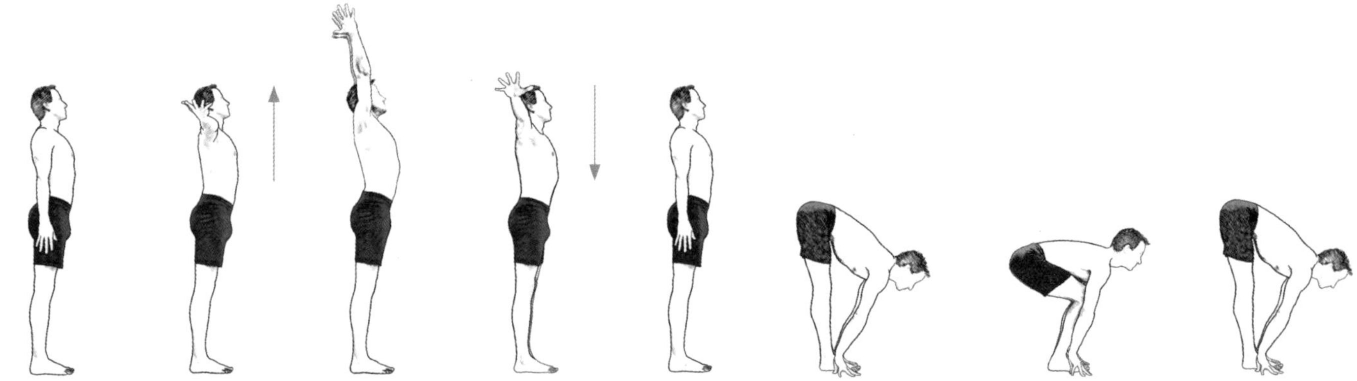
Tāḍāsana (up inhale - down exhale) Tāḍāsana Uttānāsana (bend knees) Uttānāsana

Ūrdhva Hastāsana (bow forward) Uttānāsana Prakramaṇāsana Adho-Mukha Śvanāsana (second side)

sequence components
warm-up

Warm-up Example 2 — Beginner

1. Come to hands and knees. Connect movement and breath in Mārjārāsana (Cow and Cat).
2. Transition to Adho-Mukha Śvanāsana (Downward Facing Dog pose).
3. Prakramaṇāsana (Lunge pose).
4. Parivritta Prakramaṇāsana (Revolved Lunge pose).

Mārjārāsana — Adho-Mukha Śvanāsana — Prakramaṇāsana — Parivṛtta Prakramaṇāsana

Warm-up Example 3 — Experienced

1. Adho-Mukha Śvanāsana (Downward Facing Dog pose).
2. Phalakāsana (Plank pose).
3. Lower to the floor.
4. Curl up to Bhujaṅgāsana (Cobra pose).
5. Push back to Adho-Mukha Śvanāsana (Downward Facing Dog pose).

Adho-Mukha Śvanāsana — Phalakāsana — (lower to floor) — Bhujaṅgāsana — Adho-Mukha Śvanāsana

***Note**: If you have shoulder tightness or your arms are less developed, you can bring the knees down first from Plank pose, then the hips, belly, and chest. Stronger students can lower down with the whole body remaining straight.*

Phalakāsana — (lower to knees then whole body) — Bhujaṅgāsana

sequence components
warm-up

Sūrya Namaskāra (Sun Salutation) as Warm-Up

The various forms of Sūrya Namaskāra (Sun Salutation) can be an effective warm-up for strong, seasoned students. For less experienced students, Sūrya Namaskāra can be too challenging. If you remove Caturaṅga Daṇḍāsana (Four Points Staff pose), a gentle Sūrya Namaskāra would be appropriate for a beginning level student with no injuries or other issues. However the warm-up is designed, around 3 to 5 minutes is ample time to get the body warmed up and the breath and blood flowing.

Sūrya Namaskāra—gentler version

Sūrya Namaskāra for more experienced practitioners

sequence components
standing poses

Standing Poses

No matter how experienced a student is, the first few standing poses should be simple and basic. For beginning students, introduce one pose at a time and hold for 20 to 30 seconds only. More advanced students can combine a series of two or three poses together (example on page 77). You may also choose to increase the duration of a standing pose. Holding poses for longer periods further develops strength and power as well as will and mental focus.

Basic standing poses appropriate for both beginning and advanced practitioners include any pose where both feet are on the ground and there are no twists or strong demands on balancing.

These include:
1. Vīrabhadrāsana I (Warrior I)
2. Vīrabhadrāsana II (Warrior II)
3. Utthita Pārśvakoṇāsana (Extended Side Angle pose)
4. Utthita Trikoṇāsana (Extended Triangle pose)

Poses that require balancing on one leg, such as Ardha-Candrāsana (Half-Moon pose) or Vṛkṣāsana (Tree pose), as well as revolved standing poses should come later into a standing sequence. Since these poses require greater mental focus, introducing them later into a practice allows students to "arrive" in their bodies, clear their minds, and establish their breath.

Timings in Standing Poses
Staying shorter or longer in any yoga posture creates different results. Generally speaking, holding a pose for a relatively short time (15 to 20 seconds) is easier for beginning students who are just building strength and stamina. As a student progresses, longer timings of a minute or more can further develop power and strength as well as concentration and determination. More time can also afford more space for exploration of a pose. Steady, full breathing is a key component of the practice. However, if you are designing a flow practice, keep the timings relatively brief. Either repeat a pose or recombine the same few standing poses in a different order.

Vīrabhadrāsana I

Vīrabhadrāsana II

Utthita Pārśvakoṇāsana

Utthita Trikoṇāsana

sequence components
standing poses

Transitions in Standing Poses
There are four basic methods of transitioning from the right to the left side in standing poses.

1. From Adho-Mukha Śvanāsana (Downward Facing Dog Pose)
  a. Begin from Adho-Mukha Śvanāsana
  b. Step forward to Prakramaṇāsana (Lunge pose)
  c. Come up into Vīrabhadrāsana II (Warrior II)
  d. Return to Prakramaṇāsana (Lunge pose)
  e. Step back to Adho-Mukha Śvanāsana
  Second Side:
  a. Step forward into Prakramaṇāsana with the opposite foot
  b. Then open up to Vīrabhadrāsana II
*All standing poses that follow, step out from Adho-Mukha Śvanāsana through to Prakramaṇāsana in this way.

Adho-Mukha Śvanāsana | Prakramaṇāsana | Vīrabhadrāsana II | Prakramaṇāsana | Adho-Mukha Śvanāsana

vinyasa

Vinyāsa: This more vigorous method expands on the above by adding a "vinyāsa," a portion of Sun Salutation, between the right and left side of a standing pose.

2. Vinyāsa Example — Standing Poses
  a. From Adho-Mukha Śvanāsana (Downward Facing Dog pose) step forward to Prakramaṇāsana (Lunge pose)
  b. Vīrabhadrāsana I (Warrior I) for five breaths
  c. Back to Prakramaṇāsana and through "vinyāsa" coming to Adho-Mukha Śvanāsana (Downward Facing Dog pose).
  d. Step into Vīrabhadrāsana I (Warrior I) on the second side.

Adho-Mukha Śvanāsana | Prakramaṇāsana | Vīrabhadrāsana I | Prakramaṇāsana | Phalakāsana | Caturaṅga Daṇḍāsana | Ūrdhva-Mukha Śvanāsana | Adho-Mukha Śvanāsana | (second side) | Vīrabhadrāsana I

3. Vinyāsa Example — Backbends

This is an example of another type of vinyāsa transitioning to a lying position on the floor, with the backbend Ūrdhva Dhanurāsana (Upward Bow pose).

a. Adho-Mukha Śvanāsana (Downward Facing Dog pose).
b. Jump to the front of your mat from Adho-Mukha Śvanāsana.
c. Squat and roll backward onto to your back.
d. On your back, push up into Ūrdhva Dhanurāsana.
e. Rock forward again to squat.
f. Jump back to Caturaṅga Daṇḍāsana (Four Points Staff pose).

Prakramaṇāsana   Adho-Mukha Śvanāsana   (jump to front)   Uttānāsana   (squat)   (roll back)t   (lie on back)   Ūrdhva Dhanurāsana

4. Step Wide

a. Begin by standing in Tāḍāsana (Mountain pose) at the front of your mat.
b. Bend your knees, and as you turn the body right, step wide with your right leg toward the back of your mat. You'll now be facing to the right in a wide stance with feet parallel and arms extended out at shoulder height, Pañcakarāsana (Five Rayed Star pose).
c. Turn your right foot open to point to the back end of the mat, bend the front knee coming into Vīrabhadrāsana II. Stay on this first side for 20 seconds or more.
d. Switch to the second side by straightening the front leg again, then turn the feet to parallel. Both legs are now straight with feet parallel.
e. For the second side, turn the left foot open pointing to the front edge of the mat. Right foot stays as it is.
f. Bend the left knee to form Vīrabhadrāsana II on the left side.
g. Come out by bending the knees and step the right foot back to Tāḍāsana at the head of the mat.

Tāḍāsana   (bend knees)   (step wide to) Pañcakarāsana   Vīrabhadrāsana II   Pañcakarāsana   Vīrabhadrāsana II   Pañcakarāsana   (step back to) Tāḍāsana

sequence components
standing poses

Jumping

h. This method is very similar to the Step Wide method. Begin by standing in Tāḍāsana at the center of the mat facing sideways.
i. Bend the knees and jump to a wide stance, Pañcakarāsana (Five Rayed Star pose) then initiate standing poses. From a wide stance, jump back to center.

Tāḍāsana — (bend knees) — (jump wide to) Pañcakarāsana — Vīrabhadrāsana II — Pañcakarāsana — Vīrabhadrāsana II — Pañcakarāsana — (jump feet together) — Tāḍāsana

5. Advanced Vinyāsa - Jump Back/Jump Through

These are a relatively difficult sequence of movements used to transition between floor poses. They develop strength, stamina and agility.

Simplified Version

a. While seated on the floor, bend the knees to the chest with ankles crossed then rock forward placing the hands a little in front of you.
b. Press down into the feet to lift the hips, then step or jump back to Caturaṅga Daṇḍāsana.
c. Urdhva-Mukha Śvanāsana to Adho-Mukha Śvanāsana brings you back to a position to once again jump forward to the front of your mat and squat down to sit for the second side of your seated pose.

Daṇḍāsana — (cross ankles, rock forward) — (jump back to) Caturaṅga Daṇḍāsana — Ūrdhva-Mukha Śvanāsana — Adho-Mukha Śvanāsana — (jump forward to squat) — (sit back to) Daṇḍāsana

Full Version

a. While seated on the floor, bend the knees to the chest with ankles crossed, lift the hips and feet off the floor.
b. Swing the hips and feet back through the arms to Caturaṅga Daṇḍāsana.
c. Move next to Urdhva-Mukha Śvanāsana, then Adho-Mukha Śvanāsana.
d. Bend the knees and jump forward, crossing the ankles and drawing the feet and legs as high up away from the floor as possible.
e. In this drawn up position swing through the arms to sit with legs extended.

Daṇḍāsana   Lolāsana   (swing back to)   Caturaṅga Daṇḍāsana   Ūrdhva-Mukha Śvanāsana   Adho-Mukha Śvanāsana   (jump forward through Lolāsana)   Daṇḍāsana

Standing Balances

Standing balances are poses in which you balance on one leg, such as Vṛkṣāsana (Tree pose), Ardha-Candrāsana (Half Moon pose), and Garuḍāsana (Eagle pose). These poses demand more mental focus and are best placed later in a standing sequence, after a series of more basic, stable poses.

Utthita Hasta Pādāṅguṣṭhāsana (Standing Hand to Big Toe pose) and Vīrabhadrāsana III (Warrior III) are other examples of standing balancing poses that require the muscles of the legs to be first warmed up to ensure the safety of the hamstrings.

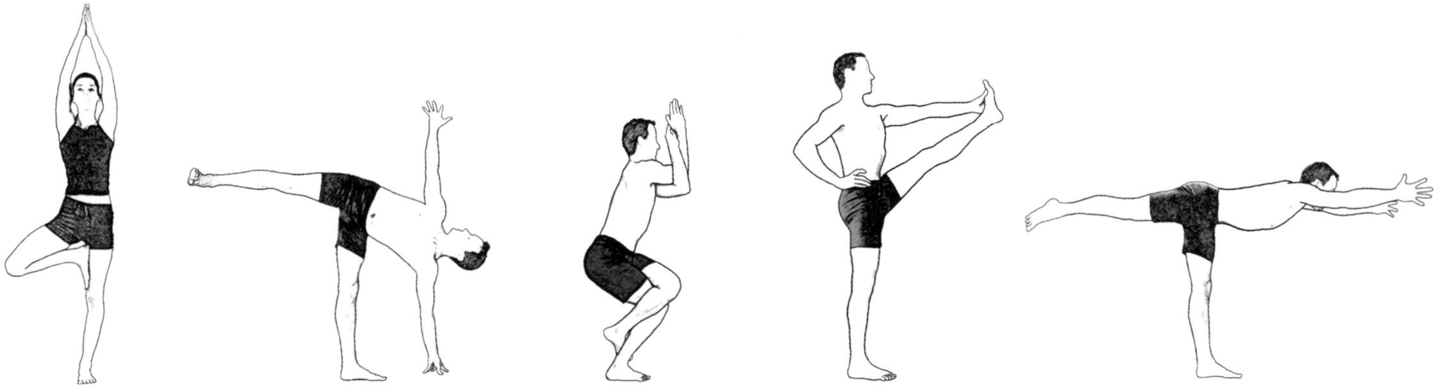

Vṛkṣāsana   Ardha-Candrāsana   Garuḍāsana   Utthita Hasta Pādāṅguṣṭhāsana   Vīrabhadrāsana III

Hip Opening Sequences

An example of initial hip opening poses in a foundational sequence would be:

1. Eka-Pāda Rājakapotāsana I prep (One Leg King Pigeon I prep - aka "Pigeon").
2. Baddha Koṇāsana (Bound Angle pose), upright version.
3. Mālāsana (Garland pose), modified.

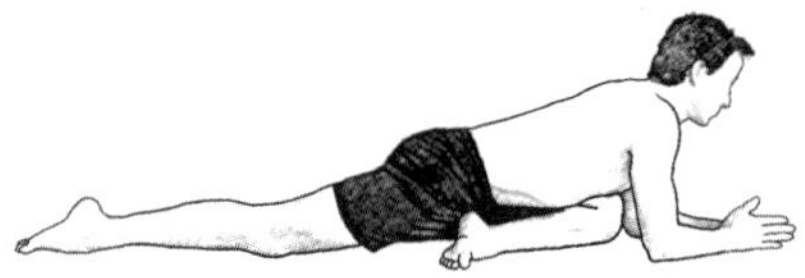
Eka-Pāda Rājakapotāsana I prep (aka "Pigeon")

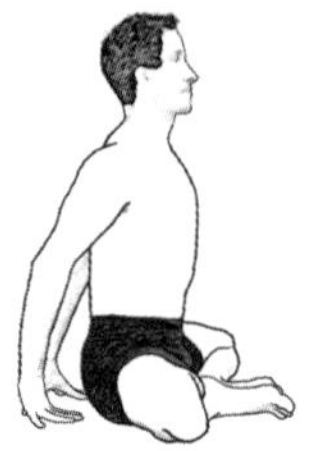
Baddha Koṇāsana

Mālāsana

After making progress in these poses over a number of practices, deepen them by bowing forward and lower.

As your hips become more open, and some of these initial poses have become easier, add poses or replace them with deeper ones.

Example:

1. Tārāsana (Star pose)
2. Agnistambhāsana (Fire Logs pose)
3. Ardha Sukhabālāsana (Half Happy Baby pose)
4. Gomukhāsana (Cow's Mouth pose)

Tārāsana

Agnistambhāsana

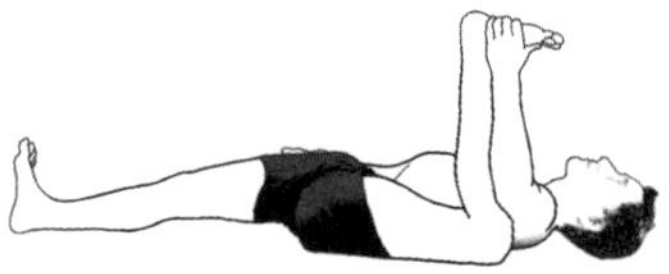
Ardha Sukhabālāsana

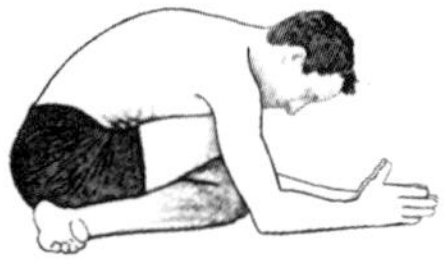
Gomukhāsana

For intermediate levels, within the standing pose section add deep lunges and bound standing poses.

Example:

1. Śīrṣāṅguṣṭhāsana (Head to Big Toe pose)
2. Āñjaneyāsana (Añjaneya's pose)
3. Baddha Pārśvakoṇāsana (Bound Side Angle pose)

Śīrṣāṅguṣṭhāsana

Āñjaneyāsana

Baddha Pārśvakoṇāsana

This gradual process of deepening the initial poses within a routine then adding additional, deeper poses to expand the scope of the hip opener section is very effective. It is a methodical way to progress and minimize any risk of injury. It also allows you to see the progress of your practice quite clearly since you're working with the same few poses over several practice sessions.

sequence components

hip opening sequences

Do all poses on both sides

Prakramaṇāsana | Sañcalanāśvāsana | Uttānāsana | Mālāsana | Baddha Koṇāsana | "Pigeon" | (bow forward) | Urasijānvāsana | Sūcīrandhrāsana | Cauraṅgyāsana

Hip Opener 1

Prakramaṇāsana | Āñjaneyāsana | Adho-Mukha Śvanāsana | Śīrṣāṅguṣṭhāsana | Uttānāsana | Mālāsana | Baddha Koṇāsana | Deep "Pigeon" | Revolved "Pigeon" | Gomukhāsana | Agnistambhāsana

Hip Opener 2

Prakramaṇāsana | Āñjaneyāsana | Adho-Mukha Śvanāsana | Śīrṣāṅguṣṭhāsana (hands bound) | Uttānāsana | Mālāsana | Baddha Koṇāsana | Tārāsana | Ardha Sukhabālāsana | Ākarna Dhanurāsana | Eka-Pāda Śīrṣāsana | Padmāsana | Gupta Padmāsana

Hip Opener 3

sequence components
forward folds

Forward Folds

Seated forward folds are often placed toward the end of a sequence as part of the cool down. They are quieting for the nervous system and help open the back of the body after backbends. They can also be woven into a sequence within the first half. For example if your routine incorporates certain arm balances that require very open hamstrings like Vasiṣṭhāsana (Sage Vasiṣṭha's pose) or Ṭiṭṭibhāsana (Firefly pose), preceding these poses with a seated forward fold such as Jānu-Śīrṣāsana (Head to Knee pose) or Upavista Koṇāsana (Seated Angle pose) can help access these arm balances more fully. Some standing poses such as Dvi-Hasta Pādāsana (Two Hands to Foot pose) or Svargadvijāsana (Bird of Paradise pose) can benefit from first opening the hamstrings in a more stable position on the floor.

Vasiṣṭhāsana

Dvi-Hasta Pādāsana

Svargadvijāsana

Ṭiṭṭibhāsana

Upavista Koṇāsana

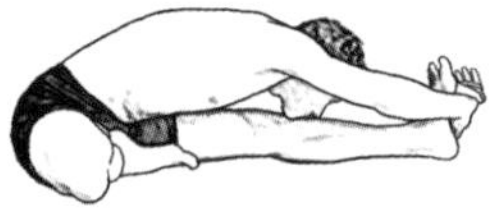
Jānu-Śīrṣāsana

Arm Balances

Arm balances demand a lot of energy and are best introduced within the first half of a sequence. As a general guideline, do more accessible arm balances before more difficult ones. Most arm balances require open hips, deep range in revolved versions, and open hamstrings.

To prepare, add poses such as these to the standing series:

1. Pārśvottānāsana (Side Stretched Out pose)
2. Prasārita-Pādottānāsana (Spread Legs Stretched Out pose)
3. Parivṛtta Pārśvakoṇāsana (Revolved Side Angle pose) variation.
4. Parivṛtta Trikoṇāsana (Revolved Triangle pose)
5. Utthita Hasta Pādāṇguṣṭhāsana (Standing Hand to Big Toes pose)

Parivṛtta Pārśvakoṇāsana

Parivṛtta Trikoṇāsana

Pārśvottānāsana

Prasārita-Pādottānāsana

Utthita Hasta Pādāṇguṣṭhāsana

Arm Balance as Peak Pose

For many of us, arm balances are the most difficult category of pose. Because of this they are good as a peak pose. After a warm-up and a series of standing poses, concentrate on the areas of the body needing preparation for your chosen arm balance. We'll use Vasiṣṭhāsana (Sage Vasiṣṭha's pose) as an example of how to sequence for arm balances.

Preparing for Vasiṣṭhāsana (Sage Vasiṣṭha's Pose) as a Peak Pose

This pose requires sustained power and extension of the legs, open hamstrings and strong work in the shoulders. It's a pose brimming with exuberance and optimism. If you are teaching a class, speak to those qualities in any opening remarks and weave them into the earlier poses.

1. To begin preparing the shoulders, emphasize the shoulder principles in Bhujaṅgāsana (Cobra pose) and Ūrdhva-Mukha Śvanāsana (Upward Facing Dog pose) in the initial warm-up.
2. Bring attention to the principles of the legs throughout the standing poses.
3. Focus on the placement of the hands and the principles of the arms and shoulders in Adho-Mukha Śvanāsana.
4. Include Pārśvottānāsana (Side Stretched Out pose), Utthita Trikoṇāsana (Extended Triangle pose) and Prasārita-Pādottānāsana (Spread Legs Stretched Out pose) for the hamstrings in the initial standing sequence.
5. Later in the sequence add Utthita Hasta Pādāṅguṣṭhāsana (Standing Hand to Big Toe pose). This can be done with the raised foot on the wall or freestanding.
6. As you get closer to your peak pose, introduce Pārśva Phalakāsana (Side Plank) then Pārśva Vṛkṣāsana (Side Tree pose). Focusing on the lift of the hips and sides of the torso as well as the working shoulder blades on the back and turning the chest upward will all be good preparation for Vasiṣṭhāsana.

Bhujaṅgāsana | Adho-Mukha Śvanāsana | Utthita Trikoṇāsana | Pārśvottānāsana | Prasārita-Pādottānāsana | Utthita Hasta Pādāṅguṣṭhāsana | Pārśva Phalakāsana | Pārśva Vṛkṣāsana | Vasiṣṭhāsana

Backbends

Backbends should come into a sequence once the upper back and shoulders are well prepared. This can be done by spending more time and focus on Bhujaṅgāsana (Cobra pose) in the warm-up. Also incorporate a few shoulder openers in the standing pose section. Poses such as Tāḍāsana (Mountain pose) with hands clasped behind the back, Uttānāsana (Standing Forward Fold pose) with hands clasped behind the back, and Utkaṭāsana (Powerful pose) with hands in reverse prayer, are especially helpful for opening shoulders. Include a variety of backbends in your sequence that work very directly with the upper back and shoulders. Basic backbends like Dhanurāsana (Bow pose), and Uṣṭrāsana (Camel pose) really focus on the shoulders. Ūrdhva Dhanurāsana (Upward Bow pose) and Dvi Pāda Vīparita Daṇḍāsana (Two Leg Upward Staff pose) work deeply in the upper back. We'll use Eka-Pada Ūrdhva Dhanurāsana (One Leg Upward Bow pose) as an example for a peak pose.

Preparing for Eka-Pāda Ūrdhva Dhanurāsana (One Leg Upward Bow Pose)
For this pose you'll want to spend adequate time opening up the upper back and chest throughout the practice.

1. Beginning in the warm-up, emphasize the alignment of the shoulders and upper back, putting more attention on Bhujaṅgāsana (Cobra pose) or Ūrdhva Mukha Śvanāsana (Upward Facing Dog pose).
2. In a standing pose such as Vīrabhadrāsana I (Warrior I), focus on bringing the head of the arm bones back, the top of the shoulders back and the lower tips of the shoulder blades forward into the body and up toward the heart. This lifts the chest and brings more of a backbend quality to the pose.
3. For further preparation, adding Ūrdhva Hastāsana (Handstand) in the first third of the sequence will inform the arms and shoulders of the work and alignment needed for the peak pose.
4. Adequate thigh opening poses before backbending opens the thighs, groins and the front of the torso.
5. Use a milder backbend such as Dhanurāsana (Bow pose) to further open the front of the body and spine.
6. As a direct preparation to the peak pose in this example, lead with Setu Bandha Sarvāṅgāsana (Bridge Building pose).
7. Perform this backbend again and extend each leg up vertically, Eka-Pada Setu Bandha Sarvāṅgāsana (One Leg Bridge Building pose).
8. Do Ūrdhva Dhanurāsana (Upward Bow pose) before moving on to the peak pose. This will further open the shoulders and establish the extension and stability needed for the peak pose.
9. Finally move to the peak pose of Eka-Pāda Ūrdhva Dhanurāsana (One Leg Upward Bow pose) lifting and fully extending one leg for a few breaths, then the other.

Bhujaṅgāsana | Vīrabhadrāsana I | (hands clasped) | Eka-Pāda Rājakapotāsana II prep | Adho-Mukha Vṛkṣāsana | Eka-Pāda Bhekāsana | Dhanurāsana | Setu-Bandha Sarvāṅgāsana | Eka-Pāda Setu-Bandha Sarvāṅgāsana | Ūrdhva Dhanurāsana | Eka-Pada Ūrdhva Dhanurāsana

Inversions

Sālamba Śīrṣāsana (Headstand) and Sālamba Sarvāṅgāsana (Shoulderstand) are most often done together with Sālamba Śīrṣāsana done first followed by Sālamba Sarvāṅgāsana. That is because Sālamba Śīrṣāsana is considered a stimulating or "heating" pose, while Sālamba Sarvāṅgāsana is considered a soothing or "cooling" pose. In this way the two are natural compliments. Both poses help to clear the mind and reduce anxiety along with other effects of stress. Always use the wall when establishing your proficiency in these poses. Only when you can comfortably stay for two minutes or more should you progress away from support.

Sālamba Śīrṣāsana and Sālamba Sarvāṅgāsana can be incorporated into a vinyāsa type routine as long as the foundation is properly set without rushing. Generally a prop should be used under the shoulders for Sālamba Sarvāṅgāsana in a vinyāsa flow sequence. Your props should be near at hand from the beginning. If you come up into either pose and things don't feel right, simply come down, reset your foundation, and come up again with mindful attention to your alignment.

Halāsana (Plow pose) is another inversion with similar benefits to Sālamba Sarvāṅgāsana. It is most commonly done in conjunction with Sālamba Sarvāṅgāsana as a resting pose or a place to reset your shoulders in the foundation. Of course there are several variations to this pose that offer their own rich experience.

Vīparita Karaṇi is another inversion that is most often performed at the wall as a restorative pose but can also be done unsupported as an alternative to Sālamba Sarvāṅgāsana.

Vīparita Karaṇi

energy balancing sequencing
grounding

Grounding

A Grounding sequence works to restore centeredness of mind and connection to the body. It can help us to refocus and settle when we are distracted, anxious, or nervous.

A warm-up is particularly important, as it sends a message to our minds and bodies to begin to relax and release tension. We can coordinate basic movements with deep, even breaths, focusing on the exhale. This will help us begin to clear and settle the mind.

Progress to basic standing poses and hold for 20 to 30 seconds while maintaining awareness on the breath. Use strong effort in the legs while letting the upper body and arms express freely with steady extension. Working the large muscles of the lower body has an insulating affect on the nervous system. Planting both feet firmly to the ground connects you to the enormous stability of the earth. Conclude the standing series with a standing forward fold such as Uttānāsana (Standing Forward Fold) or Pādāṅguṣṭhāsana (Big Toe pose). Hold for about 30 seconds. Keep the legs firm and strong while allowing the shoulders and neck more freedom.

Moving the practice to the floor for hip openers, twists and seated forward folds brings you inward and further connects you to the earth. Include inversions to further ground and quiet your mind. Move into Balāsana (Child's pose) allowing the front of your body (your most vulnerable area) to be completely protected by the earth.

Finish with Śavāsana, the pose of final surrender. Let the earth fully support your body allowing the shoulders, neck, arms and legs to soften completely. A sand bag over the top of the thighs and a blanket covering the front of the body can enhance the settling effect of this pose.

Example Grounding Sequence

Warm-up:

1. Adho-Mukha Śvanāsana (Downward Facing Dog pose)
2. Step to Prakramaṇāsana (Lunge pose)
3. Step back to Adho-Mukha Śvanāsana

(Stay in each pose 3-4 breaths. Repeat transitions two or three times)

Standing poses: (Transition between poses with Adho-Mukha Śvanāsana)

1. Vīrabhadrāsana I (Warrior pose I)
2. Vīrabhadrāsana II (Warrior pose II)
3. Utthita Pārśvakoṇāsana (Extended Side Angle pose)
4. Utkaṭāsana (Powerful pose)
5. Uttānāsana (Standing Forward Fold)

Floor poses:

1. Mālāsana (Garland pose)
2. Baddha Koṇāsana (Bound Angle pose)
3. Mārīcyāsana III (Sage Mārīci's pose)
4. Jānu-Śīrṣāsana (Head to Knee pose)
5. Paścimottānāsana (Back Stretched Out pose)

Inversions:

1. Sālamba Śīrṣāsana I (Headstand I)
2. Sālamba Sarvāṅgāsana I (Shoulderstand) or Vīparita Karaṇi at the wall

Balāsana (Child's pose)

Śavāsana (Corpse pose) 2-10 minutes (use eye pillow)

energy balancing sequencing
grounding

Do all poses on both sides

[repeat standing poses on second side]

Adho-Mukha Śvanāsana (step right leg forward) Prakramaṇāsana Adho-Mukha Śvanāsana (step left leg forward) Vīrabhadrāsana I Vīrabhadrāsana II Utthita Pārśvakoṇāsana Adho-Mukha Śvanāsana

Utkaṭāsana Uttānāsana Mālāsana Mālāsana Baddha Koṇāsana Mārīcyāsana III Jānu-Śīrṣāsana Paścimottānāsana

Sālamba Śīrṣāsana I Sālamba Sarvāṅgāsana I Balāsana Śavāsana

energy balancing sequencing
calming

Calming

A Calming sequence helps relax us if we've been pushing and striving. It will help temper any fiery tendencies. The key to Calming sequences is maintaining a smooth, relaxed breath and moving without over-efforting. Practice poses slowly or at a moderate pace. Keep your eyes and jaw soft and relaxed. Turn your gaze inward by bringing attention more and more to the sensations of the body and the rhythm of the breath.

A Calming warm-up begins with easy movement initiated by and coordinated with the breath. Repeating simple movements while establishing an even, deep breath rhythm begins to dissipate excess energy. Next cultivate a more internal direction by moving to poses that keep the visual focus downward and require more muscular engagement of the legs.

A standing sequence of strong, increasingly challenging poses harnesses mental focus. Stay in each pose 4-5 breaths, and repeat poses if desired. Avoid working aggressively. Next move to the floor for twists or hip openers. Follow with inversions, which will further bring the energy inward and sooth the mind. Finish with Balāsana (Child pose) and a long Śavāsana (Corpse pose).

> *"Yoga practice is the healing process aimed at restoring to wholeness the divine consciousness that has entered us and become fragmented through the mind, body and senses."*
>
> ~ David Frawley—*Yoga & Ayurveda, Self-Healing and Self-Realization*

Sample Calming Sequence

Warm-up:

1. In Tāḍāsana (Mountain pose), raise and lower arms with the breath x 10
2. Standing Dynamic Twists with breath x 10
3. Sūrya Namaskāra (Sun Salutation) x 2
4. Adho-Mukha Śvanāsana (Downward Facing Dog pose), hold 5-10 breaths

Standing poses: (Transition between poses with vinyāsa)

1. Vīrabhadrāsana I (Warrior pose I)
2. Vīrabhadrāsana II (Warrior pose II)
3. Utthita Pārśvakoṇāsana (Extended Side Angle pose)
4. Utthita Trikoṇāsana (Extended Triangle pose)
5. Parivṛtta Pārśvakoṇāsana (Revolved Side Angle pose)
6. Garuḍāsana (Eagle pose)
7. Prasārita-Pādottānāsana (Spread Legs Stretched Out pose - with hands bound)

Floor poses:

1. Ardha Matsyendrāsana I (Half Matsyendra's pose)
2. Gomukhāsana (Cow's Mouth pose)
3. Tārāsana (Star pose)

Inversions:

Vīparita Karaṇi (Inverted pose) 5-10 minutes (at wall), or if free standing 1-2 minutes
Balāsana (Child's pose) 10 breaths

Forward fold:

Jānu-Śīrṣāsana (Head to Knee pose)
Upavistha Koṇāsana (Wide Angle pose)
or Paścimottānāsana (Back Stretched Out pose)

Śavāsana (Corpse pose) 10 minutes (use eye pillow)

energy balancing sequencing

calming

energy balancing sequencing
invigorating

Invigorating

Invigorating sequences are strong, dynamic sequences balancing a tendency toward lethargy, inertia, or negative thinking. All sequences in this category ultimately lead to backbends, which dissolve preoccupations of the mind. They also open the heart center, and get all of the systems of the body pulsing with life.

When we feel tired or unmotivated, starting our practice can seem like a major undertaking. Begin with simple, easy movement that requires little effort or technique. Make the actions expansive and repetitive, initiated with deep full breathing. This quickly enlivens the body and clears the mind. With this surge of oxygen, blood vessels dilate, heart rate increases and prāṇa begins to flow. Progress to gentle Sūrya Namaskāra (Sun Salutations) establishing a steady, easy pace. Put emphasis on Bhujaṅgāsana (Cobra pose) or Urdhva-Mukha Śvanāsana (Upward Facing Dog pose) in this series. And again, don't be too concerned with form and technique at this stage.

Move to basic standing poses. Stay briefly but don't rush. Standing poses can be repeated or in a combination of two or three connected standing poses. Introduce arm balances after the standing sequence. These poses develop will and assertiveness as well as further warm up the shoulders.

Next move to your belly for Śalabhāsana (Locust pose), then onto your back for Setu-Bandha Sarvāṅgāsana (Bridge Building pose). Progress toward Dhanurāsana (Bow pose) and Ūrdhva Dhanurāsana (Upward Bow pose). Depending on experience, repeat these or add variations. Cool down with twists, hip openers, and forward folds. Finish with Śavāsana, staying only 5 minutes. This shorter period in the concluding posture will retain the uplifting energy of the sequence and avert sleepiness.

If you are feeling overly drained and exhausted, do a shorter practice. The important thing is to move! Begin on the floor in Balāsana (Child's pose) then move to Adho-Mukha Śvanāsana (Downward Facing Dog pose). Progress to an easygoing Sūrya Namaskāra (Sun Salutation), returning to Adho-Mukha Śvanāsana between sides rather than coming to standing. Moving and breathing is the important thing. See how you feel at this point and either finish in Balāsana or proceed as far as feels right in the above sequence.

***Note**: One of the best things we can do to uplift our state of mind and get the body moving is walk! Go out for a 10-20 minute walk in the sun or cool air and notice how things begin to shift. After that see how you feel and perhaps roll out your mat.*

Example Invigorating Sequence

Warm-up:
1. Breath of Joy (5-8 times)
2. Sūrya Namaskāra I (Sun Salutation)

Standing poses: (Transition between poses with vinyāsa)
1. Vīrabhadrāsana I (Warrior pose I)
2. Vīrabhadrāsana II (Warrior pose II)
3. Vīparita Vīrabhadrāsana II (Reverse Warrior pose II)
4. Āñjaneyāsana (Añjaneya's pose)
5. Śīrṣāṅguṣṭhāsana (Head to Big Toe pose)

Floor pose:
Kumāra Śvanāsana (Boy Dog pose)

Arm balances:
1. Adho-Mukha Vṛkṣāsana (Handstand)
2. Bakāsana (Crane pose, aka "Crow")

Backbends:
1. Śalabhāsana (Locust pose, hands clasped)
2. Dhanurāsana (Bow pose)
3. Setu-Bandha Sarvāṅgāsana (Bridge Building pose)
4. Ūrdhva Dhanurāsana (Upward Bow pose)
5. (Any additional Ūrdhva Dhanurāsana variations)

Floor pose:
Urasyubhayajānvāsana (Knees to Chest pose)

Twists:
Mārīcyāsana III (Sage Marici's pose III)

Hip Openers:
Agnistambhāsana (Fire Logs pose)

Forward Folds:
1. Jānu-Śīrṣāsana (Head to Knee pose)
2. Parivṛtta Upaviṣṭha Koṇāsana (Revolved Seated Angle pose)
3. Paścimottānāsana (Back Stretched Out pose)

Śavāsana (Corpse pose) 5 minutes

energy balancing sequencing
invigorating

Do all poses on both sides

Tāḍāsana — Breath of Joy (5–8 times) (inhale up – exhale down)

Tāḍāsana — Ūrdhva Hastāsana — Uttānāsana — (step back to) Prakramaṇāsana — Phalakāsana — (lower to floor) — Bhujaṅgāsana — Adho-Mukha Śvanāsana — (step forward) — Uttānāsana — Ūrdhva Hastāsana — Tāḍāsana

Vīrabhadrāsana I — Vīrabhadrāsana II — Vīparita Vīrabhadrāsana II — Āñjaneyāsana — Śīrṣāṅguṣṭhāsana — Adho-Mukha Śvanāsana — Kumāra Śvanāsana — Adho-Mukha Vṛkṣāsana — Bakāsana

Śalabhāsana — Dhanurāsana — Setu-Bandha Sarvāṅgāsana — Ūrdhva Dhanurāsana — Urasyubhayajānvāsana — Mārīcyāsana III — Agnistambhāsana — Jānu-Śīrṣāsana — Paścimottānāsana — Śavāsana

micro sequences

Micro sequences should be short and simple sequences that bring an immediate and beneficial shift, either lifting your energy or calming you down, ultimately bringing you into balance. Use basic, easy to perform poses that focus more on movement and less on technique or skill. Micro sequences should take only a couple of minutes to complete. They can be performed just once through or repeated several times.

Taking the theme of Grounding, Calming or Invigorating, design your sequence to quickly balance physical and mental energy, to settle yourself, or to get a dose of serenity, or a stimulating boost. (Refer to *The Yoga Practice Guide, 2* for more examples).

Micro Sequence 1 — Calming

1. Balāsana (Child's pose)
2. Adho-Mukha Śvanāsana (Downward Facing Dog pose)
3. Sañcalanāśvāsana (Advancing Horse pose or Low lunge)
4. Phalakāsana (Side Plank pose)
5. Bhujaṅgāsana (Cobra pose)
6. Adho-Mukha Śvanāsana (Downward Facing Dog pose)
7. Balāsana (Child's pose)

(Repeat second side)

Micro Sequence 2 — Grounding

1. Uttānāsana (Standing Forward Fold - holding elbows)
2. Prakramaṇāsana (Lunge pose)
3. Adho-Mukha Śvanāsana (Downward Facing Dog pose)
4. Prakramaṇāsana (Lunge pose)
5. Vīrabhadrāsana I (Warrior pose I)
6. Vīrabhadrāsana II (Warrior pose II)
7. Prakramaṇāsana (Lunge pose)
8. Adho-Mukha Śvanāsana (Downward Facing Dog pose)
9. Prakramaṇāsana (Lunge pose)
10. Vīrabhadrāsana I (Second side)
11. Vīrabhadrāsana II (Second side)
12. Step to Tāḍāsana (Mountain pose)
13. Utkaṭāsana (Powerful pose)
14. Tāḍāsana (Mountain pose)

(Repeat)

Micro Sequence 3 — Invigorating
(For somewhat more experienced practitioners)

1. Tāḍāsana (Mountain pose)
2. Ūrdhva Hastāsana (Raised Arms pose)
3. Uttānāsana (Standing Forward Fold)
4. Jump back to Adho-Mukha Śvanāsana (Downward Facing Dog pose)
5. Phalakāsana (Plank Pose)
6. Caturaṅga Daṇḍāsana (Four Points Staff pose)
7. Ūrdhva Mukha Śvanāsana (Upward Facing Dog pose)
8. Adho-Mukha Śvanāsana (Downward Facing Dog pose)
9. Jump to Uttānāsana (Standing Forward Fold)
10. Squat
11. Roll back to Halāsana (Plow pose)
12. Roll forward to Daṇḍāsana (Staff pose)
13. Pūrvottānāsana (Front Body Stretched Out pose)
14. Paścimottānāsana (Back Stretched Out pose)
15. Roll back to Halāsana (Plow pose)
16. Roll forward to squat or cross ankles
17. Uttānāsana (Standing Forward Fold)
18. Up to Tāḍāsana (Mountain pose)

(Repeat)

micro sequences

Balāsana · Adho-Mukha Śvanāsana · Sañcalanāśvāsana · Phalakāsana · (lower to floor) · Bhujaṅgāsana · Adho-Mukha Śvanāsana · Balāsana

Micro Sequence 1 — Calming

Uttānāsana · Prakramaṇāsana · Adho-Mukha Śvanāsana · (right leg forward) · Vīrabhadrāsana I · Vīrabhadrāsana II · (second side) · Utkaṭāsana

Micro Sequence 2 — Grounding

Tāḍāsana · Uttānāsana · (jump back to) · Adho-Mukha Śvanāsana · Phalakāsana · Caturaṅga Daṇḍāsana · Bhujaṅgāsana · Adho-Mukha Śvanāsana · (jump forward)

(squat) · (roll back) · Halāsana · (roll forward) · Paścimottānāsana · (roll back) · Halāsana · (roll forward to squat)

Micro Sequence 3 — Invigorating

pranayama

pranayama at the beginning of practice

Prāṇāyāma is a vast topic. My book, *The Yoga Practice Guide, Volume 2*, covers it in some detail. Here I share the basic principles of prāṇāyāma as it pertains to āsana practice.

Incorporating prāṇāyāma or yogic breathing techniques into your practice can be greatly beneficial. While a newer trend among vinyāsa flow teachers involves inserting short bursts of prāṇāyāma into a sequence during certain poses, my preference is to include prāṇāyāma at the beginning or end of a practice. In my experience this allows for better technique and integration.

Prāṇāyāma done at the beginning of practice can help to clear and settle the mind and stoke the body with prāṇa. This approach tones and balances the energy system (prāṇic body) as well as adds strength and openness to the physical postures.

Prāṇāyāma at the end of practice should aim to have a harmonizing and soothing effect. After āsana practice, the body is open and receptive, and sitting is often easier than before āsana.

Pranayama at the Beginning of Practice

Two types of prāṇāyāma I recommend for the beginning of practice are Ujjāyī (Victorious Up-Rising Breath) and Kapāla-Bhāti (Skull Shining Breath).

***Note**: Employ the bandhas during prāṇāyāma (see page 34).*

Classic seated postures for prāṇāyāma

Fig.1 Siddhāsana   Fig.2 Padmāsana

Ujjayi Pranayama

Ujjāyī is the most foundational of all prāṇāyāma techniques. Ujjāyī means "victoriously rising" or "triumphantly expanding." The Ujjāyī breath can lead us to a relaxed state of body and mind, helping us let go of fears or preoccupations and become more fully present to the moment. It increases lung strength and volume capacity, and is a powerful mover of prāṇa throughout the body.

Ujjāyī breathing has two main characteristics:
1. An action in the throat that produces the distinctive Ujjāyī sound.
2. An endeavor to maintain evenness of flow of the breath from beginning to end on each inhale and exhale, while breathing through the nose.

The distinctive Ujjāyī sound is made by lightly constricting the back of the throat, as if whispering the sound "haaaa" or as if creating fog on a mirror with your breath but keeping the mouth closed. The sound itself is not the point. Rather, you are cultivating an awareness of the breath, of both its quality and texture. This mild constriction at the base of the throat creates a slight resistance to the breath and moves the effort into the primary breathing muscle of the diaphragm. This helps you breathe more smoothly and continuously, and enables you to extend the duration of each inhale and exhale.

1. In a comfortable seated position close your eyes and start by taking a few full, easy breaths to establish yourself in your seated posture and tune into your breathing rhythms.
2. Add the slight constriction of the air passage at the back of the throat until you begin to feel the distinctive friction of Ujjāyī. Imagine that you are breathing in and out through the notch at the base of the throat rather than through the nostrils. The sound should be audible but does not need to be exaggeratedly loud.
3. Count the seconds it takes to inhale to the top of the chest, then match that as you exhale.
4. You might use a little more effort at the top of the breath in order to fill your lungs completely. At the end of the exhale, you will have to draw in or flatten your lower abdomen with slightly more effort in order to expel all of the air (Uḍḍīyāna Bandha).

5. Breathe like this for ten to twenty rounds, keeping the inhalation and exhalation even in length.
6. Then return to a natural breath. Finish by sitting quietly for a minute or so.

To Practice Kapala-Bhati

Kapāla-Bhāti emphasizes the exhale. It begins with a slower, full inhalation followed by a short, powerful burst of exhalation.

1. In a comfortable seated posture, begin an even, deep Ujjāyī breathing rhythm.
2. When you are ready, take a full inhalation then forcefully push the breath out with a quick contraction and lift of the abdomen and diaphragm.
3. Follow with a slow, full inhalation then force the breath out again. You'll find that after the short burst of exhalation, an inhale naturally follows.
4. Do eight to ten rounds of this. A round is one inhale and one exhale.
5. Return to a smooth Ujjāyī breath to rest.
6. Repeat the process three times, for three sessions of ten rounds.

***Note**: After some practice try doing Kapāla-Bhāti for 30 seconds, three times with a short break in between.*

Pranayama at the End of Practice

Nāḍi Śodhana Prāṇāyāma

This prāṇāyāma technique builds from the previous practice of Ujjāyī and works to balance the two "sides" of our energetic body. Nāḍi Śodhana is a practice of breathing alternately through the right and left nostrils but in a continuous rhythm and flow. It clears and balances the energy of the body and mind.

1. To begin Nāḍi Śodhana, block your right nostril with the thumb of your right hand in Viṣṇu mudrā and inhale through the left nostril. Also apply a tiny amount of pressure to the left nostril, but only to narrow the opening and slow the flow enough to allow for a long, steady, and smooth inhalation.
2. When you reach the top of your inhale, switch the pressure by closing off the left nostril completely and release your right nostril. Exhale through the right nostril.
3. Then inhale right, exhale left, to complete one "round."
4. Continue alternating nostrils for five rounds. I recommend counting the duration of your inhale in seconds, then match that same count for the exhale. Always keep your fingertips in light contact with the nose and let the switching back and forth be a small, subtle movement. Finish the practice with an inhale through the right nostril, then release Viṣṇu mudrā from your nose and exhale through both nostrils. Now breathe naturally for a minute or so and then lie in Śavāsana or sit for meditation.

With practice, eventually you can increase to ten rounds. Over time, Nāḍi Śodhana can be practiced continuously for several minutes. Not only can you progress to doing the whole practice for a longer duration, but also you can work to increase the length of the inhalation and exhalation, always keeping them equal.

Viṣṇu mudrā

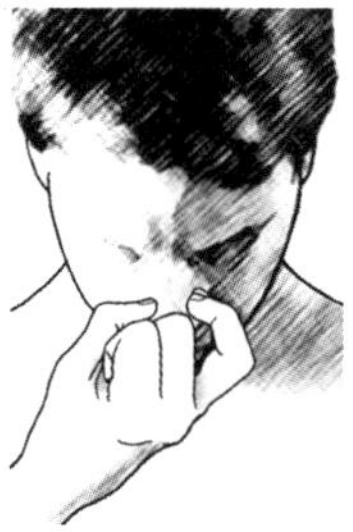

While switching nostrils, maintain contact with nose with thumb and fingers.

pregnancy

Practicing yoga during pregnancy is a wonderful way for women to stay in touch with their bodies while they go through many changes. If you have no health concerns and your healthcare provider has been consulted, then yoga practice has many benefits. If you are starting a practice for the first time, begin with a modest practice and build methodically with an experienced teacher. If you already have an established practice then you can continue as you did before pregnancy as long as there are no issues. It is prudent in the first trimester to refrain from overly aggressive practice. As your pregnancy progresses, you will become aware that modifications of many poses will become increasingly necessary for comfort. It's also advisable to avoid direct pressure on the abdomen.

Throughout pregnancy, hormones are shifting quite dramatically at times. Pay attention to how you feel and honor your needs. In the later weeks of pregnancy, the hormonal changes can make muscles and ligaments very elastic. Be aware and avoid exploiting this by stretching or twisting too forcefully.

In all, enjoy this time with your growing child within you. Surround yourself with love and peace and visualize the brightest of futures.

seniors

teachers working with seniors

There is absolutely no age limit for practicing yoga. Anyone can begin āsana practice at any point in life. If we practice wisely, we can enjoy āsana throughout our lives.

A few things those embarking on the path of yoga in their later years might consider: What is your general physical condition? Do you have any previous background in physical training? Do you have any specific health concerns or conditions? This information will be useful both to you and a teacher. At any stage of life, it is strongly recommended that you begin with lessons taught by a teacher who can monitor your needs and tailor your practice specifically to you. Teachers are there to answer your questions, address your concerns, and make sure you are always working at the level most appropriate to you.

Teachers Working with Seniors

Working with seniors can be very rewarding. I am always thrilled when seniors are interested in yoga, as it shows a willingness to step into the unknown and continue to grow. We will all get older but we never have to stop growing!

Teaching seniors can be challenging, too. Some may come to class with no previous exercise experience. This can be an intimidating experience for them. Students will wonder: What is expected? Can I do it? Will I be judged? The list of doubts and fears can be quite long. Creating a very welcoming environment will go a long way to help settle these concerns. Make sure you have thorough background information about a senior student before class begins.

If an older student has had little or no physical training, they may be weak, stiff, and not used to hearing and interpreting verbal instruction. Things that may seem easy and accessible for you may be very challenging for your older students. Keep instruction and movements as clear and simple as possible. Check in frequently to see if what you are asking them to do is clear. Use walls, chairs, and other supports for poses until your students feel confident to go without. Always return their attention to the breath. Limit the number of poses you introduce. Keep time in the pose short. It is better to have them repeat and refine the same thing a few times than to continually pile on more poses and more information. Give plenty of opportunity for breaks and rest. If Balāsana (Child pose) or sitting on the floor is a challenge, have a folding chair available. The length of initial practice sessions should be no more than 30 to 40 minutes.

A few examples of modifying poses for seniors.

seniors

example sequence

Tādāsana
(inhale up, exhale down)
(hold for 3 breaths)
Uttānāsana
(bend and straighten x 5)
(step left leg back)
Vīrabhadrāsana I
(bring hands to knee)
(step forward)
(step right leg back)
Vīrabhadrāsana I
(bring hands to knee)
Prakramaṇāsana
Adho-Mukha Śvanāsana
Bhārmanāsana
(lower to floor)
Bhujaṅgāsana
(lower to floor)
Urasijānvāsana
(stay 20-30 secs
each side)
Jaṭhara Parivartanāsana
(stay 20- 30 secs
each side)
Śavāsana

seniors
recommended syllabus

***Note**: This is not a sequence! Appropriate for beginning students as well.*

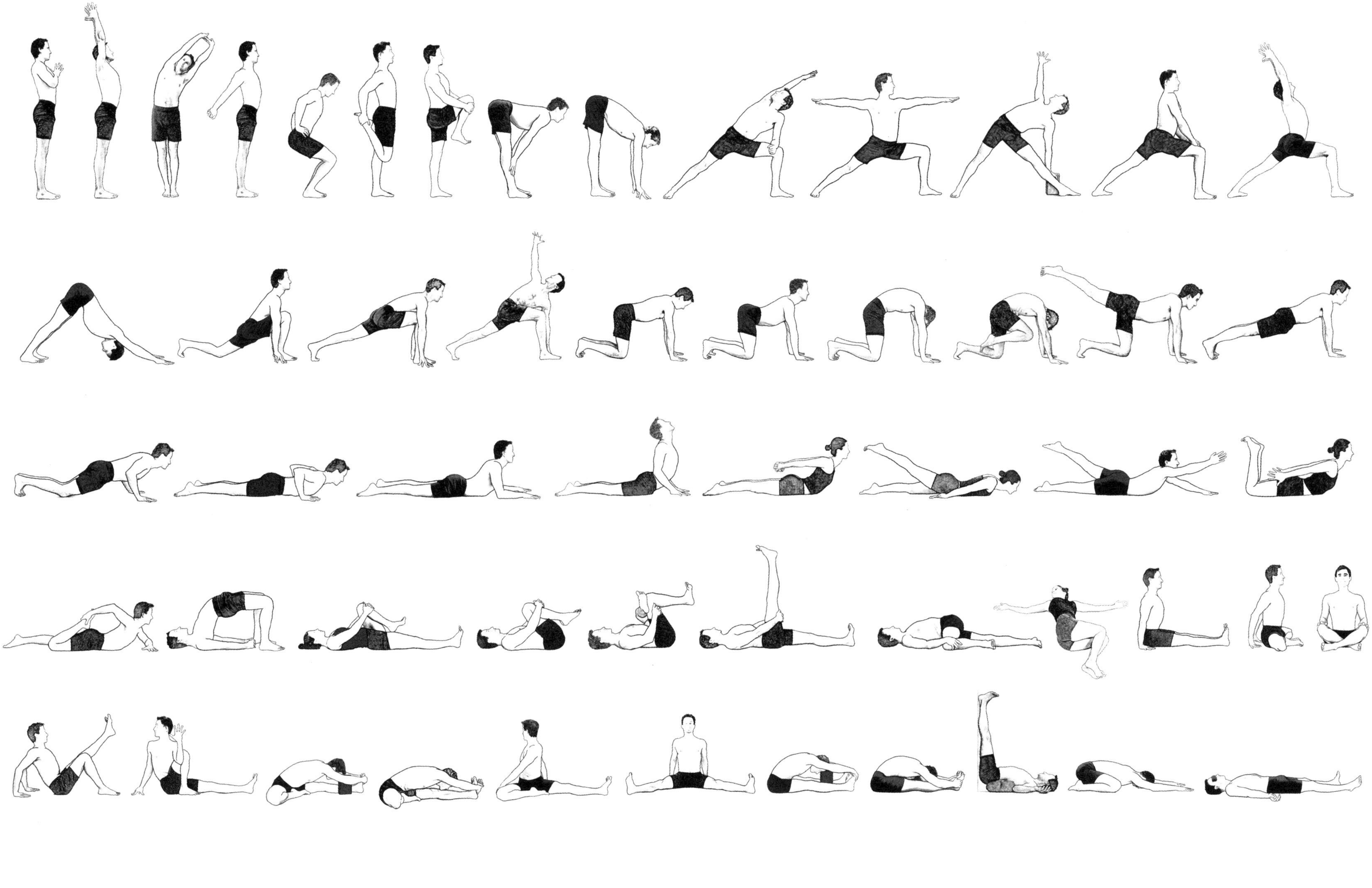

asana syllabus
standing poses

● beginner ● intermediate ● advanced

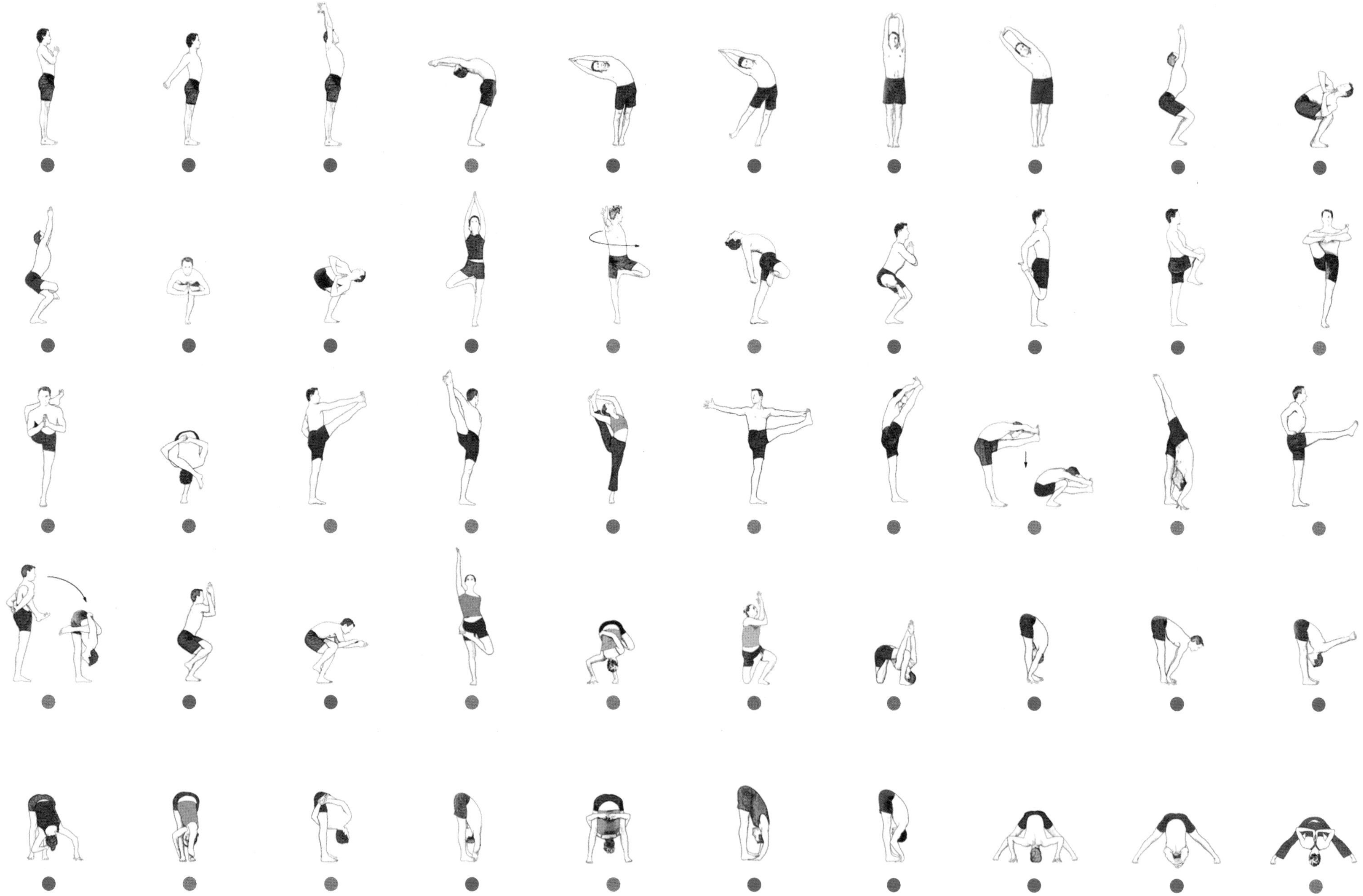

asana syllabus
standing poses

● beginner ● intermediate ● advanced

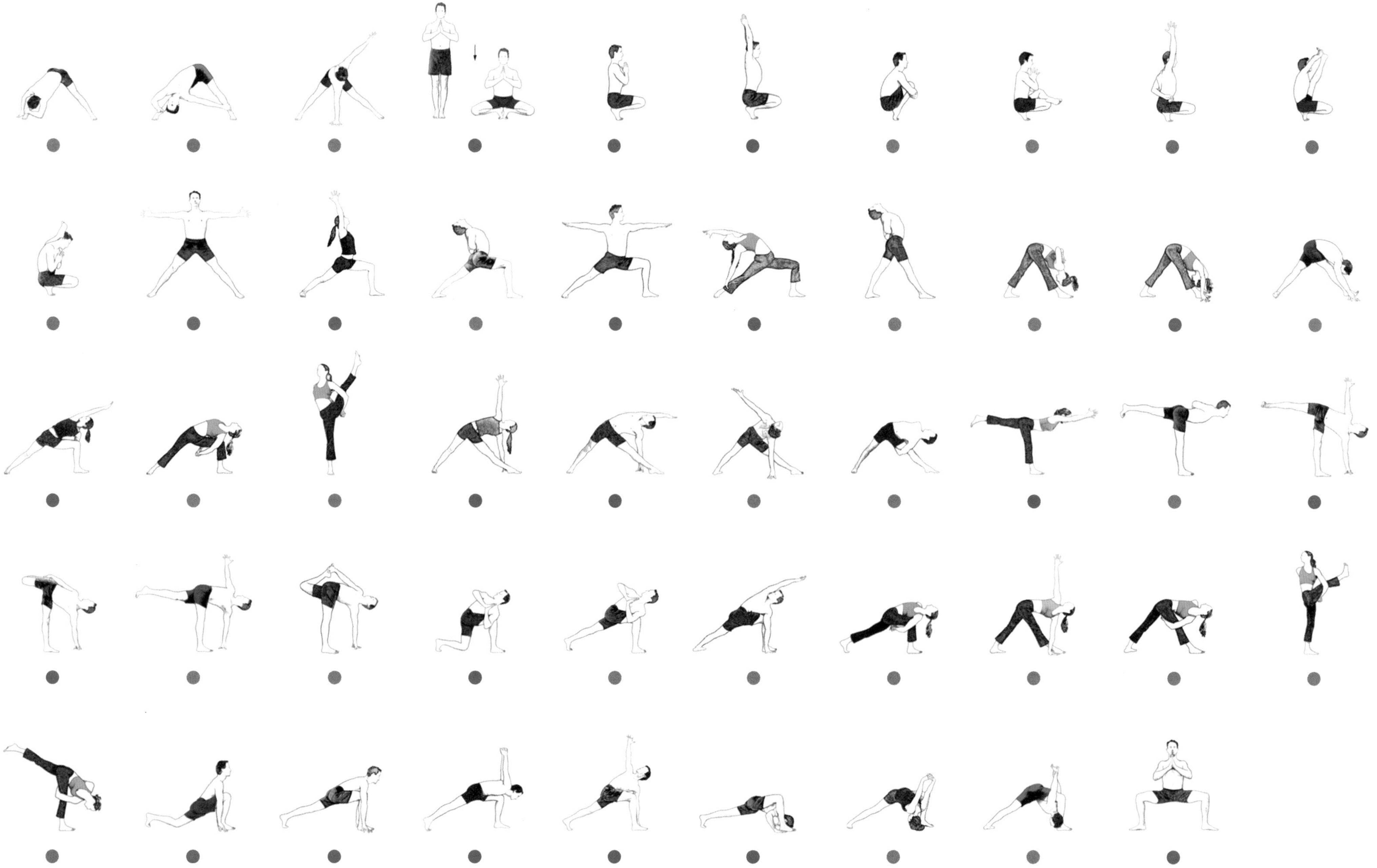

asana syllabus

floor poses, forward folds, supine twists

● beginner ● intermediate ● advanced

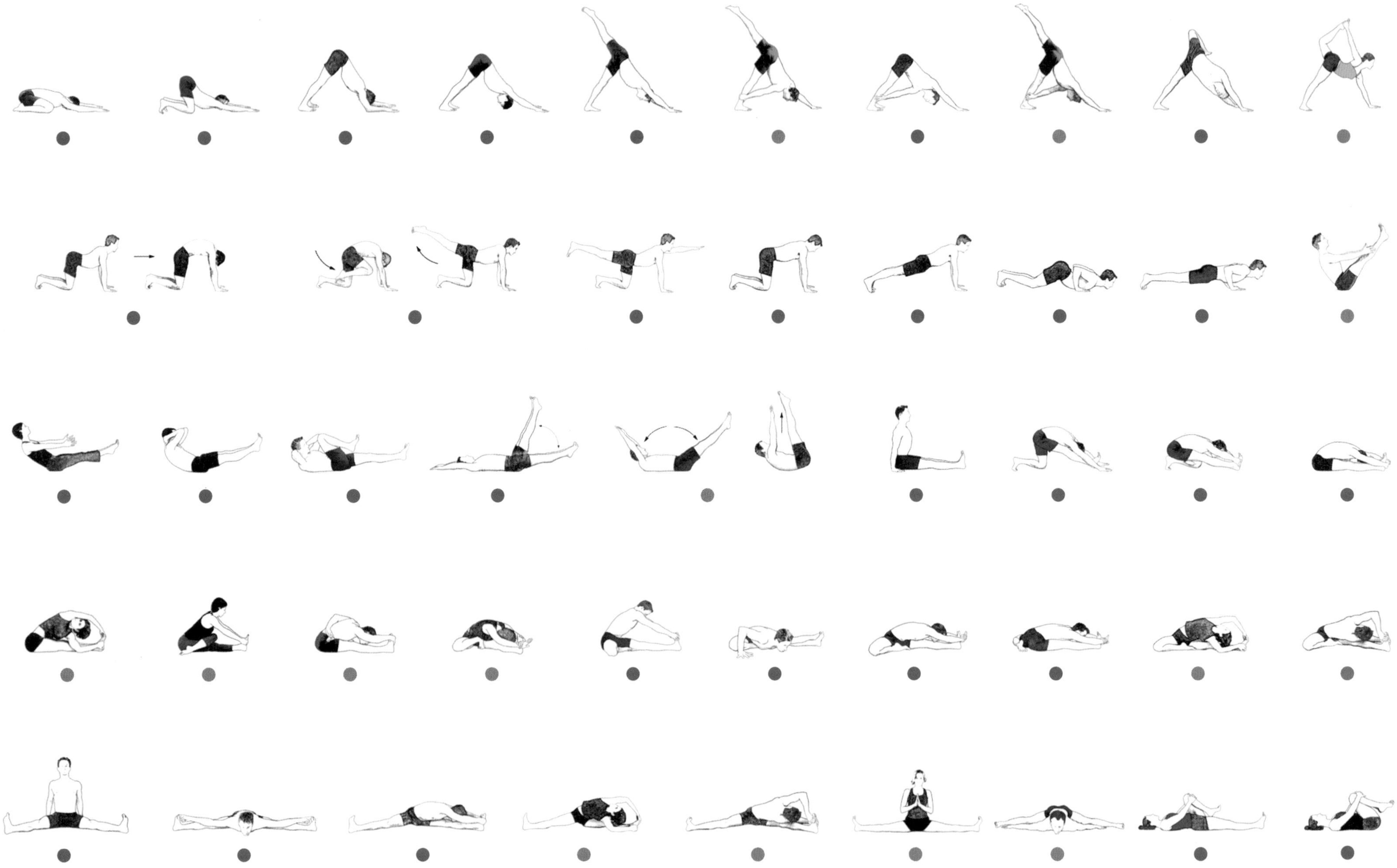

asana syllabus
floor poses, forward folds, supine twists

● beginner ● intermediate ● advanced

asana syllabus
hip openers, seated twists

● beginner ● intermediate ● advanced

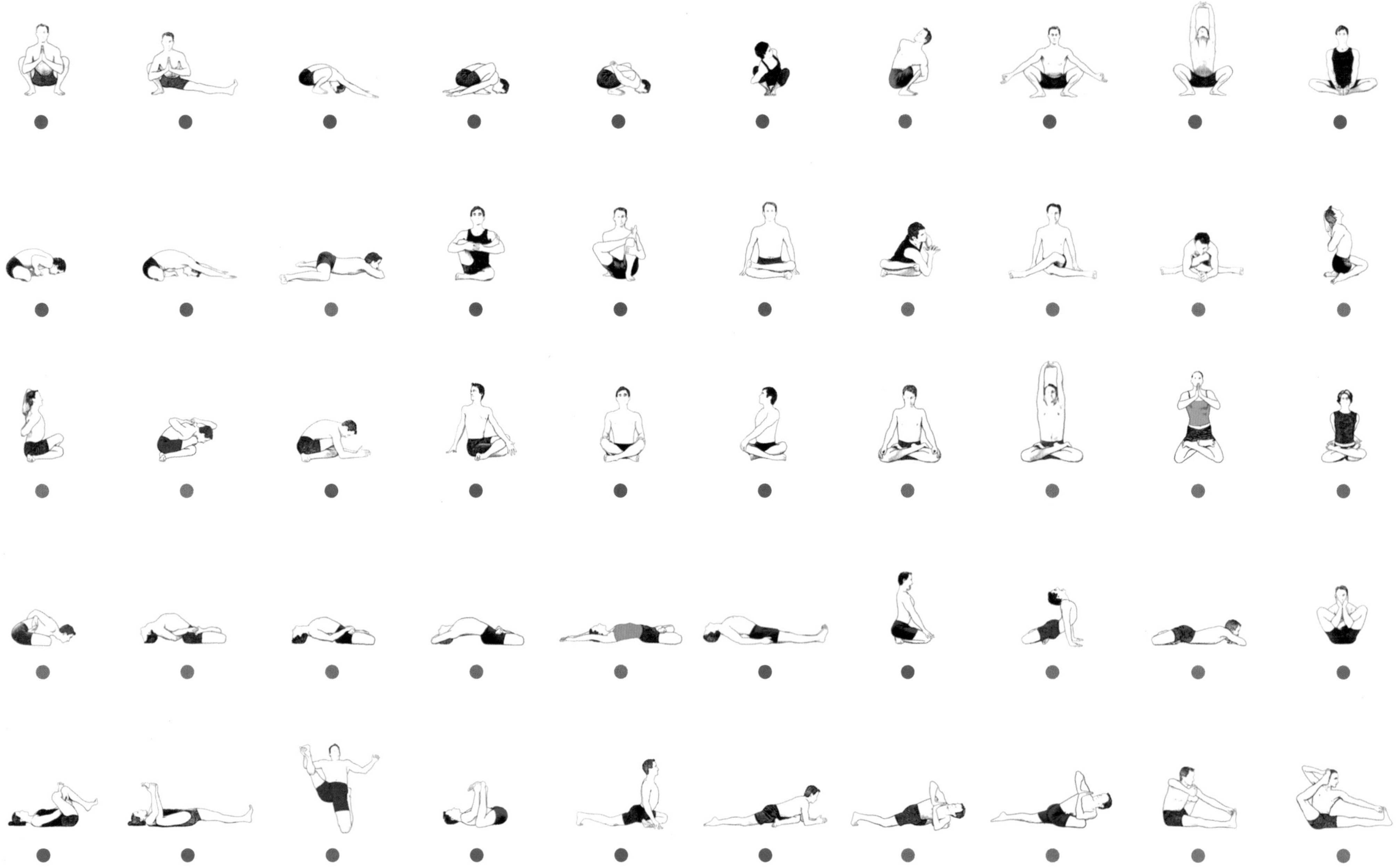

asana syllabus
hip openers, seated twists

● beginner ● intermediate ● advanced

asana syllabus

arm balances

● beginner ● intermediate ● advanced

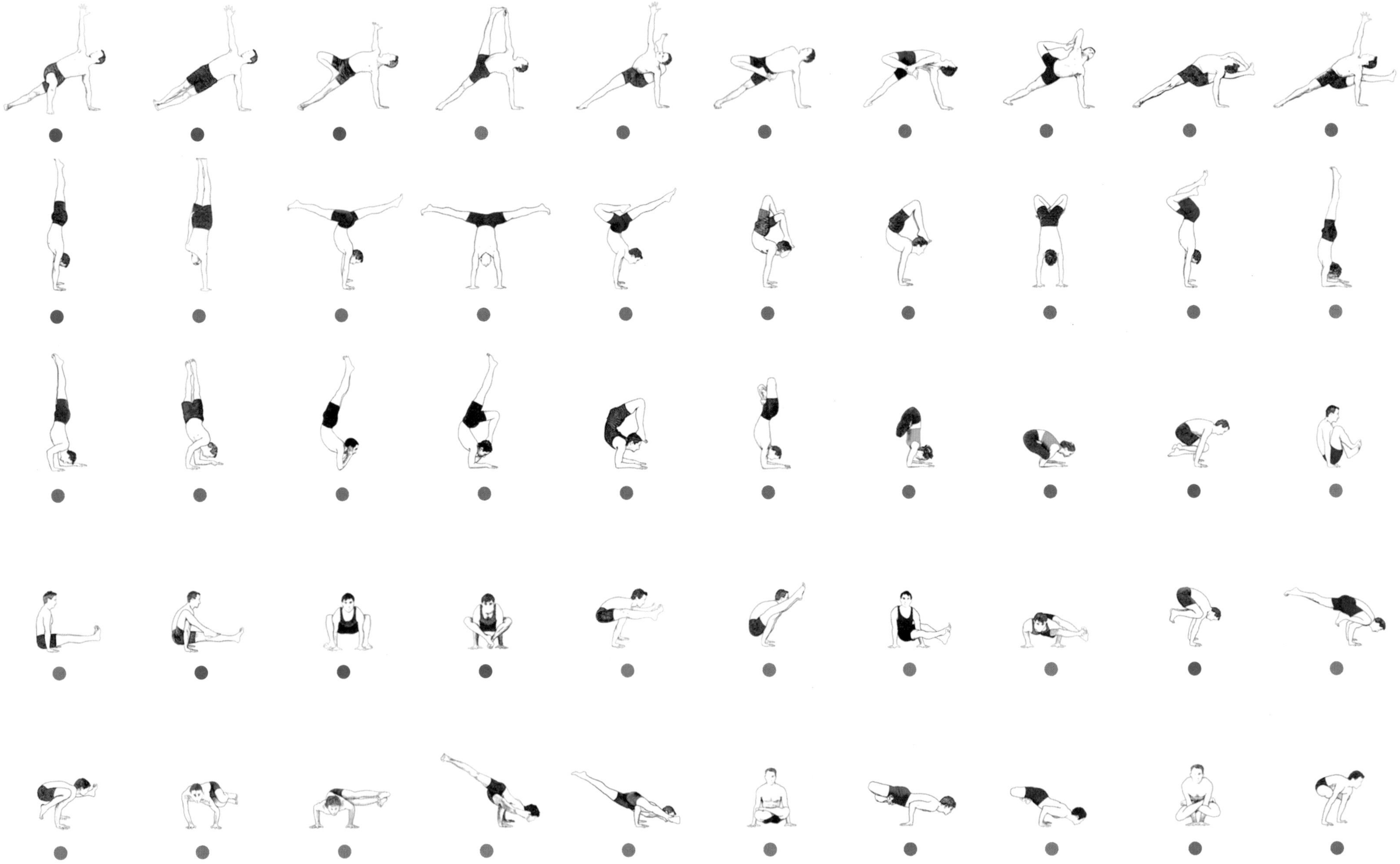

asana syllabus

arm balances

● beginner ● intermediate ● advanced

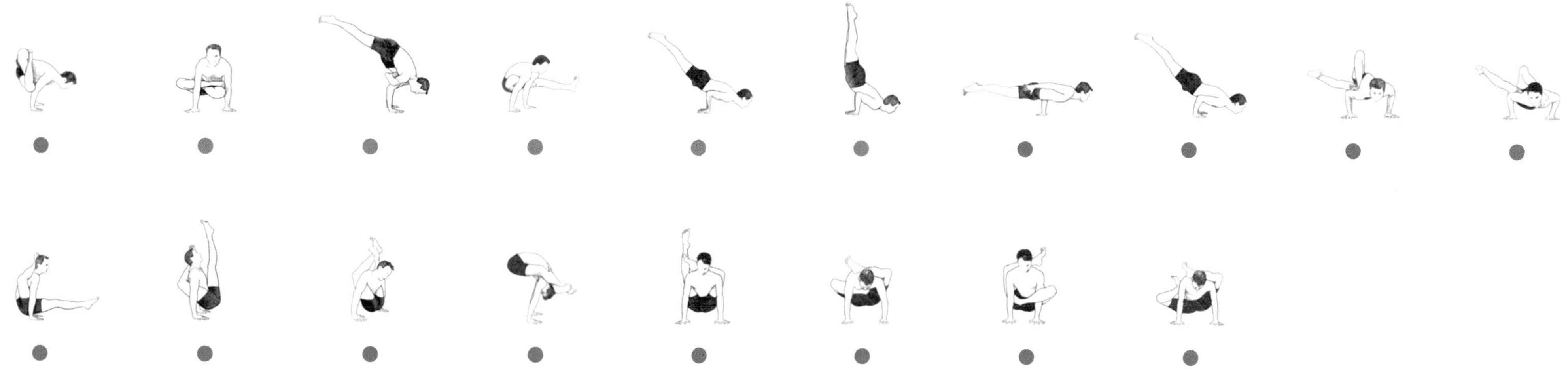

backbends

asana syllabus

backbends

● beginner ● intermediate ● advanced

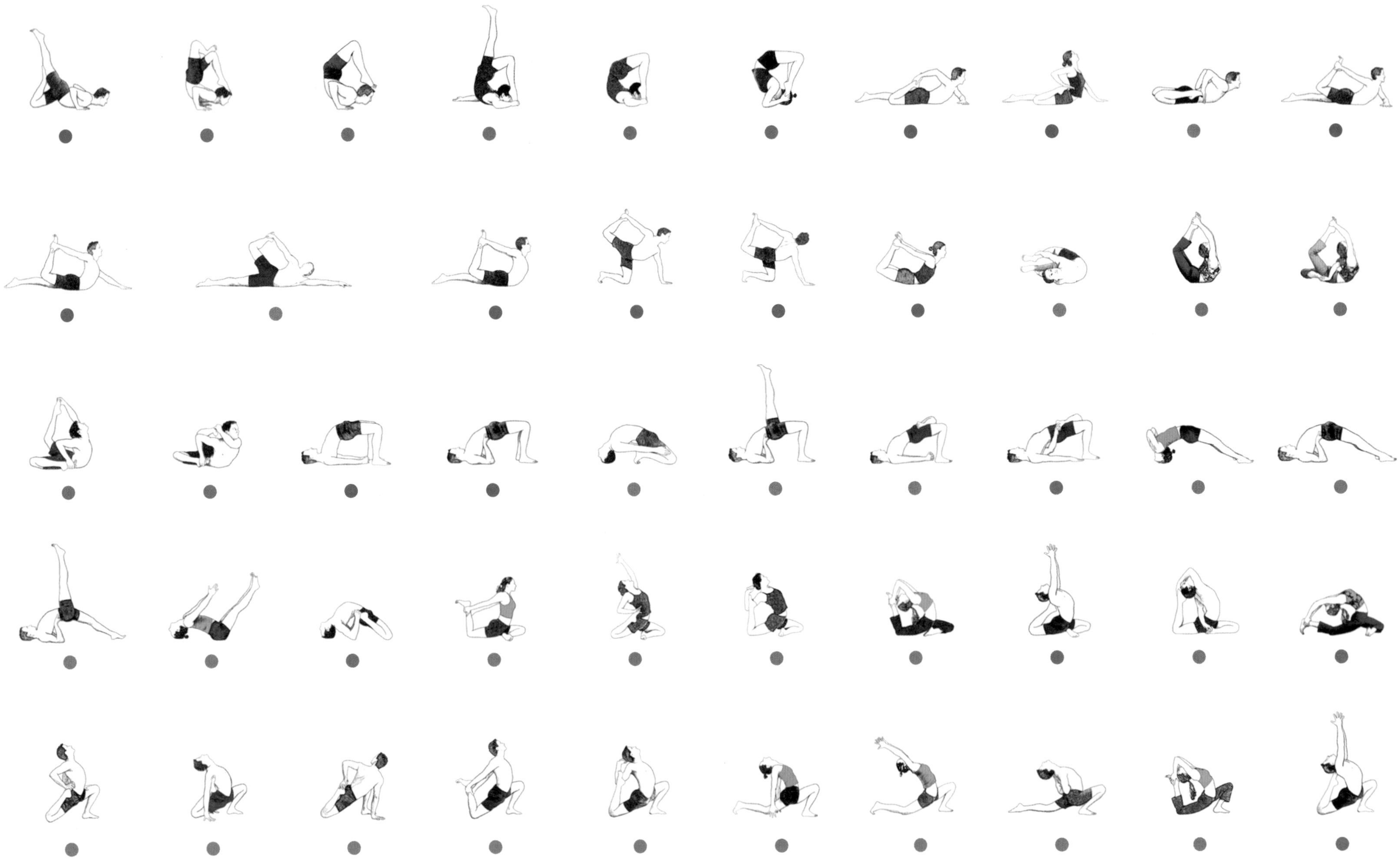

asana syllabus
backbends

● beginner ● intermediate ● advanced

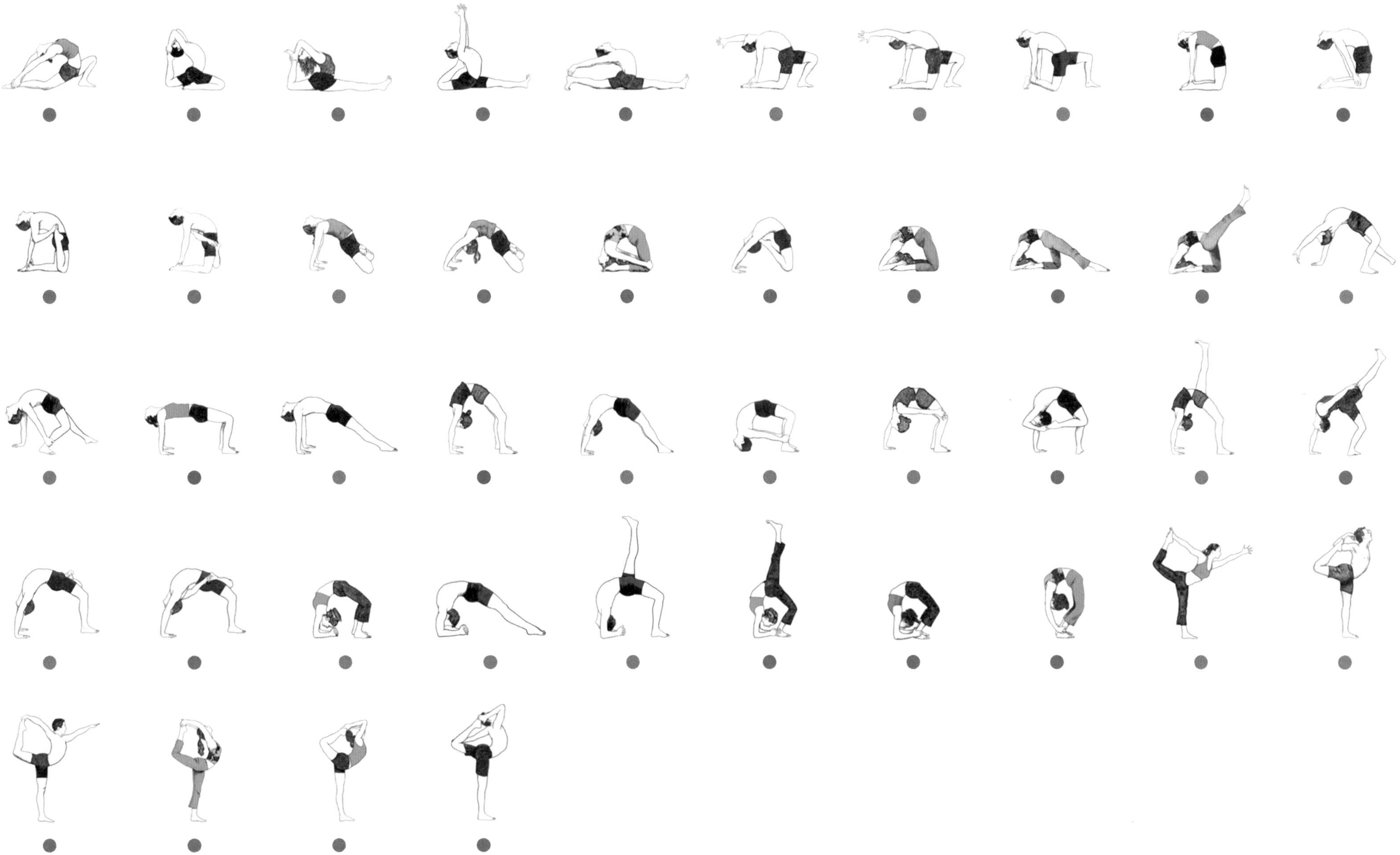

asana syllabus
inversions

● beginner ● intermediate ● advanced

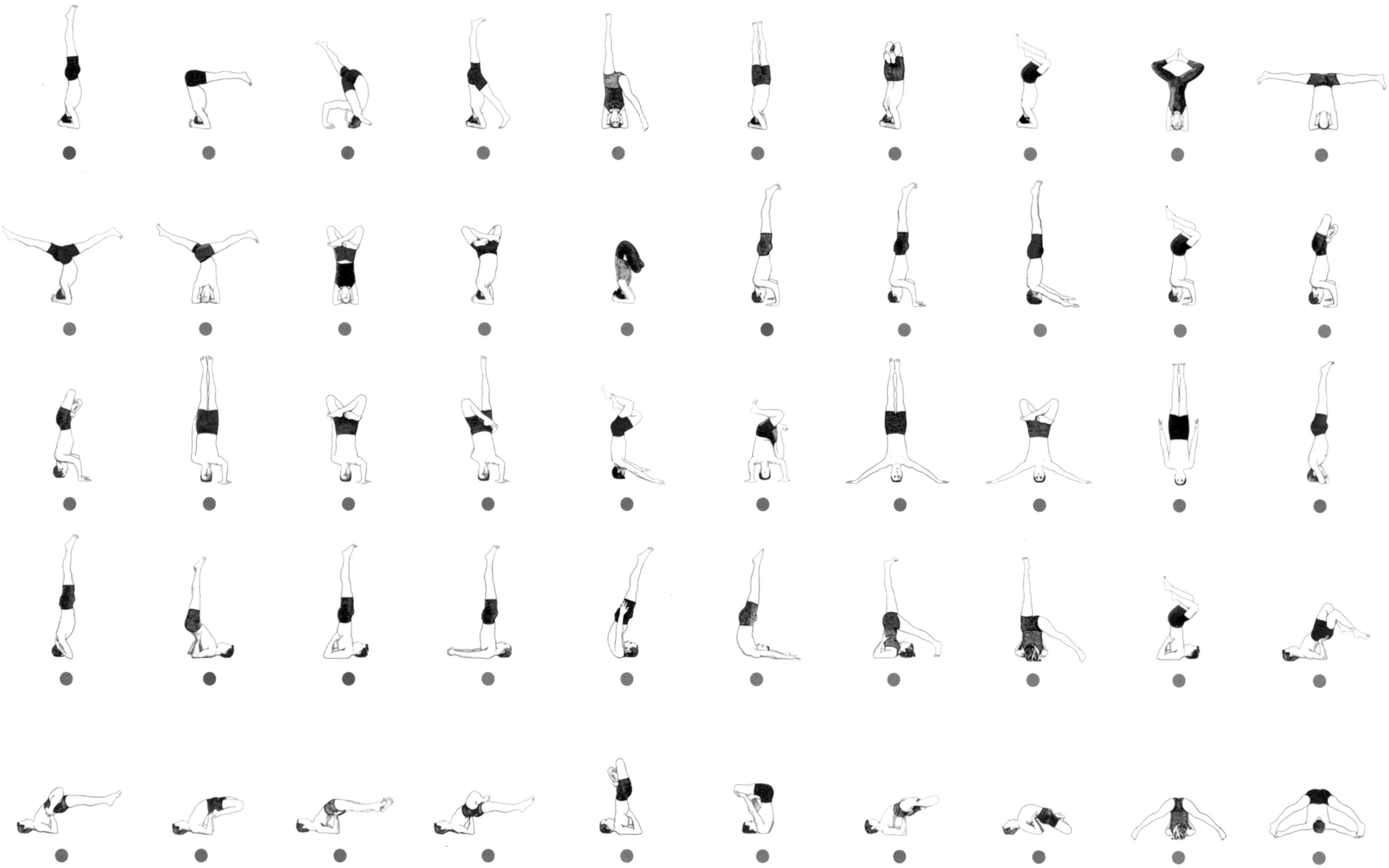

asana syllabus
inversions

● beginner ● intermediate ● advanced

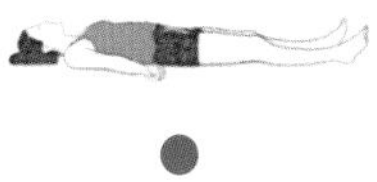

What if my wrists hurt in:

1). Adho-Mukha Vṛkṣāsana (Handstand)

Discomfort in the wrists in handstand usually means we have lost both Muscular Engagement and Energetic Extension in the hands. This will compress the wrist joint. Extend the fingers fully and press them strongly into the floor. This will distribute the weight more through the whole hand and open the wrist.

2). Ūrdhva Dhanurāsana (Upward Bow pose)

The same issue here as with handstand: bring more Muscular Engagement and Energetic Extension to the hands. Another issue can be stiffness in the upper back, making it difficult to extend the arms fully and bring the shoulders up over the wrists. This puts the wrists at an acute angle causing pain. The solution is to use a wedgeboard under the hands or a tightly rolled blanket at the wall to open the angle of the wrist and make it easier to straighten the arms.

What if my lower back hurts in:

1). Dhanurāsana (Bow pose)

Overly engaging the buttocks and lower back muscles as you initiate this backbend can result in painful compression of the lumbar spine while diminishing flexibility in the upper back. The solution is to begin with Bhujangāsana (Cobra), establishing as much length in the waist and side of the body as possible, then curl the upper back and shoulders (keep the buttocks and lower back neutral). Maintaining the work in the upper back, keep that the focus and reach your hands to the feet. Holding the feet, press them back and extend up through the shins to the balls of the feet. The chest is broad and expansive. The upper arms lift away from the floor. The buttocks and lower back will engage but no more than the upper back.

2). Uṣṭrāsana (Camel pose)

It can be helpful to think of Uṣṭrāsana as Dhanurāsana (Bow pose) on your knees. The key is to lengthen the side of the body up away from the hips and curl the shoulders, focusing on the area of the upper back. Maintain the breath! The tailbone anchors toward the floor yet the buttocks remain relatively neutral. Once the hands are on the heels of the feet, press the hands down to reinforce the lift of the chest. The upper arms press back and the chest lifts up and forward. Check again that you haven't clenched the buttocks!

3). Ūrdhva Dhanurāsana (Upward Bow pose)

Pain in the lower back in Ūrdhva Dhanurāsana comes from the same tendency to overwork the muscles of the buttocks and try to drive the backbend from the pelvis. This is especially so if you have difficulty straightening the arms. The solution is to soften the buttocks and lower the hips a little. This will allow the groins to soften. With that, lengthen the tailbone and draw from the pubic bone to the navel. This lengthens the lower back and avoids lumbar compression.

What if my knees hurt in:

1). Dhanurāsana (Bow pose)

Usually knee pain in this pose is from a lack of Muscular Engagement in the form of hugging the shins toward the mid-line. When you hold your feet and before you come up into the pose, spread your toes as much as possible and even turn the feet slightly out. This creates the needed Muscular Engagement in the lower leg. Maintain that and keep the knees outer hip width apart, then extend back and up through the legs. The hands pressing a little toward each other will help the shins hold the mid-line.

2). Vīrabhadrāsana II (Warrior II)

Check the position of your front foot and knee. Is your foot turned in or out instead of straight forward? The knee should be directly over the ankle. Make sure it isn't over to one side or the other or forward over the toes. Any of these misalignments can put strain on the knee joint.

What if my ankle hurts in:

1). Utthita Trikoṇāsana (Triangle pose)

This situation occurs when there is a lack of Muscular Engagement in the legs and not enough drawing in toward the vertical mid-line with the feet and lower legs. The result is the base of the shin pushes forward creating discomfort in the ankle joint. The remedy is to get the base of the shin to move back (toward the vertical mid-line, or toward the back foot). One remedial method is to roll a mat or use a wedge board and place it under the front half of your foot. This reduces the angle of the ankle joint and allows the base of the shin to move back more easily. Using a prop like this will take away the pain and can be used until you learn to consistently draw the base of the shin back and maintain the integrity of the ankle joint.

2). Vīrāsana (Hero pose)
Discomfort in the ankle and top of the foot in this pose is due to either tightness of the fascia around the front of the ankle and foot or the angle of the foot or both. A rolled blanket can be placed under the ankles to alleviate pressure. The heels should hug in against the outer hips and the top of the toes should be flat on the floor. Spread the toes wide away from the hips with emphasis on spreading the little toes. This will also help most knee discomfort.

What if my hamstrings hurt in:
1). Uttānāsana (Standing Forward Fold)
Back off the pose a bit and refresh the principles of Muscular Engagement of the legs including pressing the lower legs toward the vertical mid-line. Inwardly rotate the upper, inner thighs back and apart. Add the descent of the tailbone and lengthen the legs straight. When these are back in balance the strain in the hamstring should disappear. Also try a block under the hands.

2). Utthita Trikoṇāsana (Triangle pose)
Refer to page 21. To those details add a focus of descending the tailbone (or bringing it slightly but firmly under) while maintaining a degree of inner rotation of the back leg. Remember that in all standing poses the front leg has a predominance of outer rotation and the back leg a predominance of inner rotation. The two are in balance. Use a block under the front hand.

3). Jānu-Śīrṣāsana (Head to Knee pose)
When strain is felt particularly at the insertion or attachment of the hamstring of the straight leg you need to refresh the principles of the legs and pelvis (refer to pages 19 and 38). Manually do inner rotation of the straight leg making sure to ground the thighbone down afterwards to keep the rotation. Reach through the heel and press it down to engage the hamstring. Next, press out through the ball of the foot (refer to page 27). With these actions maintained and the whole leg energized, lengthen the torso up out of the pelvis and bow forward. Maintain a slight descent of the tailbone. When these actions are in balance the hamstring is safe and protected and can stretch evenly.

My hamstrings are tight. How do I stretch them?
Of course to safely stretch the hamstrings, refer to the principles of the legs in the first half of the book. An effective method to gradually open the hamstrings is by working in Uttānāsana (Standing Forward Fold). Place your feet outer hip width apart. Bend the knees with the finger pads on the floor or blocks. Working the principles of the legs, begin to straighten the legs to whatever degree is comfortable, pause, then bend them again. Repeat that several times. Keep the hands in contact with the floor throughout. If you do Uttānāsana this way every time you practice, your hamstrings are sure to become more open. On the floor, seated forward folds can be done in a similar way. Using the example of Paścimottānāsana (Seated Forward Fold), begin with legs somewhat bent. Emphasize the inner rotation of the upper inner thighs and deepen the groins. Tight hamstrings tend to cause the tailbone to over-tuck and tilt the top of the pelvis back. Bow forward and reach as far down the leg toward the feet as comfortable. Pause a couple of breaths, then come back up. Repeat. Each time you practice try to reach further down the leg and eventually work toward the legs becoming more straight. Remember that opening the body is a process and the time it takes will vary from person to person.

What if I feel shoulder strain in:
1). Ūrdhva Dhanurāsana (Upward Bow pose)
Discomfort in the shoulder usually occurs when the head of the upper arm bone gets pushed forward toward the front plane of the body. This makes the shoulder joint very unstable. To reset the shoulders, come back down to the floor. Place your hands in preparation to push up. They can be as wide as the edges of the mat, wrists even with your ears. Draw the armpits down toward the floor (back plane of the body). Move to the top of the head. Reaffirm the armpits back. That sets the head of your humerus deep into the shoulder socket. Maintain that and press up. Encourage the outer edge of the shoulder blades back. Difficulty in straightening the arms can also make it difficult to set the head of the arm bone. In this case refer to the above answer to wrist pain in Ūrdhva Dhanurāsana. Changing the angle of the wrist makes it easier to straighten the arms and set the humerus in the shoulder socket.

2). Piñca Mayūrāsana (Forearm Balance)
Pain in the shoulder in Piñca Mayūrāsana comes from the same misalignment described above for Ūrdhva Dhanurāsana (Upward Bow pose): the head of the arm bone has pushed forward away from the back plane and destabilized the shoulder joint. Come back onto the knees and forearms. Place the forearms parallel to each other and shoulder width apart. With the elbows

directly under the shoulders, sink the chest toward the floor. This brings the shoulder blades onto the back and sets the humerus deeply into the shoulder socket. Maintain that and lift the hips and knees to a Downward Dog position. Keep the shoulders set and step the feet a few inches closer toward the arms bringing the hips higher. Kick up from here. Reaffirm the head of the arm bone back into the shoulder socket (toward the back plane) and the chest moves toward the front plane. Legs joined together and fully extended, move the tailbone into the body.

3). Bhujaṅgāsana (Cobra pose)
To reset the shoulders bring your chest back down to floor. Lengthen the legs and tailbone and keep the muscles of the buttocks soft! Lengthen the side of the torso forward from the hips to the armpits. Maintain the length and bring the shoulders forward and up away from the floor. Now the top of the chest and collar bones are "looking" forward and the upper back is slightly curled. Maintain that curl of the upper body while pressing down into the hands. Avoid overly contracting the lower back and buttocks as this diminishes length in the torso, creates rigidity, and makes the shoulders less mobile.

I can't breathe in seated twists or revolved standing poses.
Let's take Ardha Matsyendrāsana (Half Matsyendra's pose) as the example. If you find it hard to breathe in a twist two things have happened. You have lost the inner body extension of the torso and you have twisted leading with the front of the body and pushed your belly forward. So, before you enter your twist, lean your torso back a little away from the bent leg. Lengthen up out of the pelvis with the torso. Lead with the inhale! The chest is raised enough so that the lower ribs and upper abdomen are clear of the bent leg. Maintain the length of the torso and extend your tailbone down. Lift the lower belly up and in. Think of the pelvis as a bowl. As you lengthen the tailbone down you draw the lower abdomen back toward the inner bowl of the pelvis, then up. The lower back will fill in with this action as the sides of the waist also draw back (toward the back plane). With these actions holding steady, exhale into your twist focusing on the waist. The upper body and shoulders would be steered with the arm that's over your raised bent-knee leg.

Can I practice through an injury?
Most injuries in yoga are the cumulative result of some misalignment done repeatedly in practice. To continue to practice without exploring the root cause will result in further injury. Laying off practice to heal is always advisable, yet when you get back on your mat and continue to do the same thing as before, you will get the same result. The most constructive thing is to determine what pose or type of pose led to the injury. Once that is determined, carefully analyze what principles are involved in performing the pose, then see which of those principles may have been under-done or even over-done. There will be a period of re-patterning the body in these poses so take your time. Be patient and methodical. Once you understand the principles involved in safely performing the pose, the same pose that precipitated an injury will now help to heal it.

What if I am always losing my balance in Tree pose or other balancing poses?
Any standing balance can be done using the wall. This is a useful method to add stability to your pose while you build strength and understanding within the posture. For example, Vṛkṣāsana (Tree pose) can be done by placing one hand or even just one finger on the wall. With Vīrabhadrāsana III (Warrior III) stand facing the wall at a distance so when you come up into the pose you can fully extend the arms bringing the fingertips to the wall. Ardha-Candrāsana (Half Moon pose) can be done with the back body supported at the wall. You are then more able to focus on the principles of the legs and pelvis and can more easily open the chest and shoulders.

If yoga is ultimately a spiritual practice, why does Haṭha yoga focus so much on the body?
It is through our bodies that we interface with the world around us. Our body is the most immediate and direct experience we encounter. Every physical, mental or emotional event is registered in our bodily tissues. The Tantric[15] developers of Haṭha yoga recognized this fact and saw that the physical body should then be the initial focus of a system of practice aimed at deep self-transformation.

Tantric philosophy and practice has many overlaps with other spiritual teachings such as the model of the koshas[16] from Vedanta[17] and the eight limbs or aṣṭaṅga[18] from Patanjali. These concepts describe how we are multilayered beings that require a variety of practices to address each facet of our being. Haṭha yoga traditionally uses āsana and cleansing practices to address the physical body, prānāyama to address the energetic or prānic aspect, meditation and study (of scripture and philosophy) for the mind, mantra and visualizations to access higher wisdom, and deep meditation to reveal the light of consciousness at the core. It was also recognized that no aspect of our being is separate from another so each aspect (and each type of practice) has its influence on the other.

Should I continue to practice when I am sick?
We'll assume this question refers to things like the common cold. If you are sick, wait until you are better and your symptoms have passed. Rest is what you need most!

Can I practice when I am having my period?
Ultimately this is a personal choice based on how you feel during this time of the month. Traditional Ayurveda tends to advise that this time be honored as a period of rest and rejuvenation. Āsana or other forms of exercise that may affect the flow of the cycle are not advised. It is suggested that this be a time for gentle meditation and positive reflection.

In headstand, where should the head be placed?
If your neck has an even, normal cervical lordosis (slight forward curve) then the very top of the head is placed on the floor. If you were to draw a line from the top of the ears to the top of the skull, that would be the spot. If your neck tends to be more flat (less curve or a reverse curve - kyphosis) then you'll need to shift to a spot more forward towards the hairline. This position encourages more lordosis or forward curve of the cervical spine. Review page 26 for neck alignment.

How much weight should be on the head in headstand?
The answer varies depending on the headstand. For Sālamba Śīrṣāsana I, the best long-term results come from using the arms and shoulders a little more when first learning. Eventually progress toward less use of the arms and shoulders until the head takes the majority of the weight and the arms are used minimally for lateral stability, sort of like the training wheels on a bicycle. This gradual shift comes about as you can energetically extend consistently through the center mid-line of the body, both down into the floor with the head and up from there straight through to the feet. The more you can extend the neck and reach to the crown of the head, while holding the mid-line with fully charged and extended legs, the less the arms and shoulders need to work. When you have this balance of actions, the neck muscles are surprisingly soft and the pose will feel light with little effort.

In Śīrṣāsana II (or tripod headstand) the arms are in a different position and do need to work more firmly to stabilize the body. That is also why this pose is usually held for shorter durations. Śīrṣāsana II is most used as a transitional pose between other arm variations in headstand rather than for long holds.

Why do we roll to the right to come out of Śavāsana?
I have come across a few interesting hypotheses as to why coming out of Śavāsana (Corpse pose) is most often done to the right. Yet it isn't really all that complicated. There is a Sanskrit word, *pradakshinā*, which literally translates as "to the right" and describes any entrenched tradition. In many cultures (including Indian) the right is consider auspicious or good while the left is considered unlucky or even malicious. So chalk it up to superstition or tradition, rolling out of Śavāsana to the right is just how it's been done. So if you are inclined to finish your practice on the left side, it won't affect your karma, your health or anything else. Go for it!

Do I have to change my diet and lifestyle to do yoga?
The answer is no. You can eat whatever you like and do whatever you like and practice yoga. Yet, as discussed in the last paragraph on page 11, as you practice more you may begin to make new choices. You may become more sensitive to behavior or things you habitually eat that aren't so good for you. You may begin to shift into a new pattern that better supports your long-term health. There are of course other considerations to diet such as quality of food, ethical questions around eating meat or dairy, refined sugar etc. There is plenty of information on optimal diet out there and some of it is confusing and conflicting. Traditionally a vegetarian diet is encouraged. Since animals are sentient beings, not eating meat was an ethical consideration to avoid negative karma and be in more balance with the living world. Ultimately it comes down to a personal choice. There are no requirements or conditions to practicing yoga.

endnotes

1 (Page 5) Ayurveda, meaning "the science of life," is the ancient healing system of India. It implements primarily diet, herbs and a range of spiritual practices including yoga.

2 (Page 5) Biomechanics is the study and analysis of the structure and function of biological systems. It is concerned with the internal and external forces acting on the human body and the effects produced by these forces. Another way to put it is that biomechanics aims to understand the mechanical cause-effect relationships that determine the motions of the human body.

3 (Page 21) An isometric muscle contraction, or static exercise, is one in which the muscle fires but there is no movement of the limbs. There is no change in length of the muscle, and no movement at the joints.

4 (Page 28) Research conducted by the Body-Mind Centering group, speaks to how the musculature of the hands and feet (Lumbricals) creates a substantial difference in energetic flow relating to breath and overall body function and openness. *Lumbrical Movement of the Feet and Hands: Sensory Integration from Core to Periphery* by Annie Brook, Exploring Body-Mind Centering, North Atlantic Books, 2011.

5 (Page 30) Kinesthetic awareness encompasses the body's abilities to coordinate motion (such as pitching a baseball) and the body's awareness of where it is in time and space.

6 (Page 30) Proprioception is the ability of your central nervous system to communicate and coordinate parts of your body with each other.

7 (Page 43) This refers here to the iliopsoas, iliacus and psoas major muscles. The iliopsoas and iliacus are deep, internal muscles connecting from the upper, inner thigh bone at the lesser trochanter, to the anterior inferior iliac spine (inside front of the pelvis). It continues as the psoas major connecting up to the five lumbar vertebrae. This group of muscles (commonly called the psoas collectively) create a tremendous stabilizing link from the legs, through the pelvis up to the lumbar spine. The psoas is the integral physical component of mula bandha and uddiyana bandha.

8 (Page 53) Restorative yoga is a vast topic and one that would warrants another whole book. My other two books, *The Yoga Practice Guide, Volume 1* and *2* include more on this topic. I recommend Judith Lasater's book, *Relax and Renew*, Rodmell Press, 2011. Also, *Yoga, The Path to Holistic Health* By B.K.S. Iyengar, Dorling Kindersley LTD, 2014.

9 (Page 54) It's important to "warm-up" the joints and muscles slowly and methodically before introducing strenuous or complex poses. Moving the body in this way stimulates the secretion of *synovial fluid*, a clear fluid secreted by membranes in joint cavities, tendon sheaths, and bursae, and functions as a lubricant. This process gets the body ready for more demanding movement.

10 (Page 55) *Grounding, Calming* and *Invigorating* correlate with the Ayurvedic model of the Doshas: *Vata, PItta, Kapha. Grounding, Calming* and *Invigorating* are antidotes to Doshic imbalance.

11 (Page 56) Contemporary vinyāsa styles derives from Ashtanga Yoga or Ashtanga Vinyāsa, developed by Patabi Jois in the mid-1960s. Ashtanga Vinyāsa is an athletic and demanding āsana practice comprised of a number of preset sequences that progress through levels of increasingly more advanced and demanding poses.

12 (Page 60) The lymphatic system is a network of glands and vessels. Its primary function is to transport lymph, a clear, colorless fluid containing white blood cells that rids the body of toxins, waste and other unwanted materials such as bacteria and is closely tied to immune system function.

13 (Page 60) The vagus nerve is one of the largest nerve systems in the body. It is actually two cranial nerves that extend from the brain stem and connect down to the viscera. The vagus nerve is used to regulate a variety of body functions including the heartbeat, blood pressure and muscle movement associated with breathing as well as aspects of digestion.

14 (Page 62) During exercise, blood flow through tissues changes dramatically. The overall effect of exercise on circulation is to greatly increase the blood flow through exercising muscles, up to 20 times greater than through resting muscles, and to keep blood flow through other organs at a low value, just adequate to supply their metabolic needs.

15 (Page 106) Tantra: A way of showing the unseen consciousness in form through specific words, diagrams, and physical postures. Includes esoteric symbolism and magic paralleling Western Alchemy. Kashmir Shaivism (a branch of Tantrism): states that everything in the universe has both male and female qualities. The attraction between them produces the ultimate union of the universe.

16 (Page 106) The Five Koshas - Layers of Consciousness: According to this view of human experience, there are five layers or dimensions by which we experience our self and the world. They range from the outer, physical body through to our deepest spiritual aspect.

17 (Page 106) Vedanta: An umbrella term used for the traditional ancient Vedic teachings of India. The core premise being that every human being is innately divine. And the ultimate goal of life is to manifest this inherent divinity.

18 (Page 106) Aṣṭaṅga - The Eight Limbs: Are a set of eight distinct practices forming a blueprint for controlling the mind's restlessness to cultivate lasting peace and connection to Divine source.

acknowledgements

I would like to thank Kimi for her help with the text. Jana and Mike for proof reading, Melina for all her great design skills and Jade for the beautiful cover shot. I'd also like to thank all of my students who have taught me so much about being a teacher. To Mother Earth who sustains us all.

about the author

Bruce has authored four books about yoga and conducts workshops and trainings both nationally and abroad. He is an accomplished healer and possesses detailed knowledge and skill in yoga therapeutics.

He was first introduced to yoga in his high school gym in the late '70s in Rome, Italy, by his enlightened basketball coach. From that time on he became interested in meditation, Asian philosophy and martial arts. He studied fine art in Baltimore and Paris. While in college, he had the good fortune to become a student of several master martial arts teachers and over a period of 15 years earned black belts in three styles.

Bruce became an Art Director and had a career of several years in multinational advertising agencies overseas. It was during his last year in the business in Melbourne, Australia, that he rediscovered his yoga practice. He was so inspired that he left advertising and began studying yoga in earnest.

Bruce studied several styles of yoga, particularly Iyengar and Ashtanga yoga, with master teachers of both styles. In 1999 he was introduced to Anusara yoga and John Friend. John soon became his primary and most influential teacher. Anusara yoga merged Bruce's love for a graceful and powerful physical practice with a life-enhancing and heart-centered spiritual practice. He was a certified Anusara yoga teacher for some years and is now independant.

Bruce's sensitivity and humor give him the ability to connect with each student, and make his teachings personal, transformative and rich. Bruce is continually studying all aspects of yoga practice and generously shares his knowledge and discoveries. Through his teaching, he helps others find the best in themselves and experience the creativity, passion and soul that is the art of yoga.

additional books

The Yoga Practice Guide

Dynamic Sequencing for Home Practice and Teachers

The Yoga Practice Guide is a uniquely detailed manual helping practitioners clearly visualize and understand all the components of developing an effective, balanced, home practice from beginning to advanced level. Where most books on yoga merely touch on the subject of sequencing, The Yoga Practice Guide offers a wide variety as well as a unique "Modular System" for customizing your practice. All sequencing is designed to open the body methodically based on sound therapeutic principles. The over-sized format allows most sequences to be displayed across facing pages. The book lies flat making it easy to use.

Key features:

- Methodically guides practitioners through safe, efficient, well-rounded practices that target specific areas of the body from beginning to advanced.
- All sequencing designed to open the body systematically based on sound therapeutic principles.
- Unique "Modular System" section helps you customize your own practice with confidence.
- Perfect class guide for teachers of yoga.
- Clear and accurate illustrations listing all Sanskrit names.
- Step-by-step guide with several sequences in each level.
- Therapeutic, restorative and "chair" yoga sequences.

The Yoga Practice Guide 2

Sequencing and Pranayama for Energy Balancing

Our bodies are a total energy system. Yoga practice can be a powerful influence for balancing and integrating this complex network. *The Yoga Practice Guide 2* has fully illustrated yoga practice sequences designed to help you harmonize and optimize your energetic flow, creating radiant health and a strong and supple body and mind. Includes details on the chakra system, in relation to yoga practice, as well as in-depth guidance for various forms of prāṇāyāma, or breath work. Through practice we become more deeply seated within the heart so our gifts may be offered more fully to the world!

Key features:

- Detailed sequences for higher energy.
- Sequences for calming and cooling.
- Sequences for balancing and integration.
- Restorative and therapeutic sequences.
- Extensive section on prāṇāyāma.
- Sections on the chakra system and Kundalini Shakti.
- Each section has from beginner to advanced level.
- Clearly illustrated with Sanskrit names.
- Oversized format and spiral bound for easy reference.
- Heavy paper stock stands up to daily use.
- Perfect for students and teachers alike.

The Yoga Asana Index

A Complete Index of Hatha Yoga Postures

The Yoga Asana Index is a celebration of the beauty and form of hatha yoga postures. With over 500 detailed illustrations accurately showing āsanas and mudrās, it is one of the most complete and comprehensive collection of yoga postures anywhere. Each pose is accompanied by its Sanskrit name plus a complete glossary of both the English and Sanskrit names.

The Yoga Asana Index is organized into standing poses, floor poses, forward folds, hip opening poses, seated twists, arm balances, backbends, and inverted postures. Twenty-three mudrās represent the most important and powerful hand gestures in the practice of yoga.

Key features:

- One of the most complete indexes of hatha yoga postures anywhere.
- Over 500 different poses and mudrās clearly illustrated with Sanskrit names.
- Full Sanskrit to English and English to Sanskrit glossary.
- Audio CD helps you learn the correct Sanskrit names.
- Spiral binding opens flat for easy viewing.
- Heavy paper makes it hold up to use.
- Invaluable reference resource for any student or teacher of yoga.
- A great companion to *The Yoga Practice Guides 1 & 2*.